Praise for
Remove, Replace, Restart

Career journeys today are more like winding, multileg road trips than the traditional ladder of yesterday. The formulas and three-step processes from the past no longer apply. Instead, *Remove, Replace, Restart* offers a highly relatable and practical guide for all of us to reflect on our careers and take action to make "work" work.

—CHRISTOPH SCHWEIZER, Chief Executive Officer,
Boston Consulting Group

A fresh and stimulating look at a field that so often seems to be dominated by processes and templates, Christian's book brings humanity and wisdom to bear in equal proportions. Written in a cheerful, practical, and engaging style, this is a fresh and welcome addition to the resources available to those of us who might otherwise flounder in the face of career challenges and crises.

—GUY ASHTON, Chief Executive Officer, Meyler Campbell

Every leader goes through transitions in his or her life. This book is a wise and practical guide to navigating these transitions successfully. Christian writes both thoughtfully and engagingly, making this a very refreshing and hugely valuable book for each of us.

—HARISH BHAT, Brand Custodian, Tata Sons;
marketer, author, and columnist

To deal impactfully and professionally with all the ambivalences and challenges in the business world requires constant development in leading others and leading oneself. Christian Greiser shows, with a light touch, how we actively and courageously decide to look at, reflect upon, and question ourselves. Drawing from his unique perspective through working with leaders, his extensive business insights, and his personal experience, he invites us

to push our own boundaries consistently and to reframe the accountability of the leadership role in a strategic, disciplined, and also encouraging way.
—DR. THELSE GODEWERTH, member of the Board of Management, and Labour Director, Rolls-Royce Power Systems AG

I have been fortunate to work with Christian on my own career journey, and I am so pleased to see that he has decided to write this book so that everyone can benefit from his wisdom and insight. I recommend this book to every leader and aspiring leader because they will enjoy Christian's ability to interweave his experience, case studies, and good humor into practical advice.
—ANDREW BELSHAW, Chief Executive Officer, Gamma Communications plc.

Zen and the Art of Motorcycle Maintenance: An Inquiry into Values is a timeless classic where Robert Pirsig studies the concept of quality. I have read and reread it several times over decades. Recently, I discovered Christian Greiser's *Remove, Replace, Restart*, a book that struck similar chords in my mind. However, its topic is not quality in general but the quality of your career. The book is relevant for everybody who puts value on conscious career planning. It enables you to detect an overzealous inner driver that might push you to burnout. It teaches you to turn breakdowns into insights that allow you to build not just a great career but a beautiful life. My copy is already quite tattered from frequent rereading and doing the helpful exercises, and I have gifted this wonderful book to several friends who are shaping their own careers or those of their children, coworkers, or clients.
—PROF. DR. FRANZ J. GIESSIBL, nanoscience pioneer, University of Regensburg

Christian Greiser's book certainly shifts gears! It outlines a simple and easy-to-follow pathway of how to switch from the passenger's seat to the driver's seat by mastering your professional goals while aligning them with what truly fulfills you. It encourages you to try and test, to experiment with who you could be and what life could look like. While backed by hard facts, studies, and numbers, it encourages you to trust the somewhat intangible gut feeling every leader has at some stage that "something is not quite right" and convert it to a powerful tool of self-steering.

—CHRISTINA VIRZÍ, founder and Chief Executive Officer, Virzí & Co KMG

If you want to achieve more and overcome the typical challenges of a top management career, this book is the ideal read. The real-life case studies shared from a gifted coach perspective will softly urge you to do some introspection. Christian has beautifully intertwined the merits of the six Rs, particularly *remove, replace,* and *restart* to *rejuvenate* and continue to grow and pursue one's dream.

—ANIL JHANJI, Chief Commercial Officer, Tata Steel UK Limited

Many leaders are at an inflection point, learning how to lead their organizations and progress their careers after so much volatility and uncertainty in our lives the past few years. Christian Greiser's book provides exactly the guidance needed to navigate this time, pairing a lighthearted rendition of relatable stories with encouragement to reflect and self-realize a path forward via his six Rs approach.

—LAURA JULIANO, North American Operations Practice Lead,
Boston Consulting Group

Think career guides are difficult to digest and even more difficult to put into practice? Not in this case: you are invited to observe others' ineffective behavior in entertaining case studies as a charming mirror in which . . . I started recognizing my patterns almost by accident. And the suggested coping strategies are just as easy to digest: they come within the case study, supplemented with a quick explanation of the underlying model. [*Remove, Replace, Restart*] feels like a beach read . . . while being great food for thought at the same time.

—DR. TOBIAS KEITEL, member of the Corporate Board of Management;
President and Chief Executive Officer, Voith Hydro

Many have looked to tackle the challenge of present-day management: at the core, executives are simply overwhelmed. Christian Greiser's book presents the challenge and solutions in an engaging, easy-to-read, and motivating way. It is a pleasure to read and, more importantly, the examples are salient and relevant, leaving a lasting impression to jump-start personal change for the reader.

—DIANA DIMITROVA, Managing Director and Partner,
Boston Consulting Group

Remove, Replace, Restart is truly career- and life-changing! The hands-on advice in the book is so insightful and impactful that it changed the way I think about my job, my career, and what I want to achieve in the next five years. The case studies gave me a new and fresh perspective on my management style and my inner workings. I absolutely recommend the read to anyone, irrespective of which stage of their career and life they are at—the book has ton of insights for everyone. A must-read!

—TIMUR YUMUSAKLAR, President and Chief Executive Officer,
F. Schumacher & Co.

Christian Greiser's book is a wonderful and fun-to-read guide for everyone's journey through the career jungle—where, more and more, straight-line careers will be the exception rather than the rule. I wish I could have read it earlier: I turned from a "Wall Street lawyer" to a "management consultant" to a DeepTech start-up founder during my career. With Christian's book, a lot of self-doubt and unstructured thinking could have been avoided. If you are considering a career change and are holding this book in your hand, then you are lucky. Go out and try new things—and this book will be a great advisor all the way.

—TRINH LE-FIEDLER, Chief Executive Officer and founder, Nomitri

You might be skeptical at first when you get your hands on the 300th career guide. But this book is really different, especially because of the case studies, in which Christian Greiser comes to surprising conclusions with very unusual analyses of clients' problems. While reading, one sometimes catches oneself anticipating the usual career advisor's answer, and then stumbles over a sentence that takes a day to think about. Great book, best read in small stages so that you give yourself enough time to reflect thoroughly on what you have read.

—FREDUN MAZAHERI, Chief Risk Officer and Chief IT Officer,
Pictet Europe

In a time where 95 percent of companies find that they will fundamentally change over the next five years and two-thirds of their leaders assume that they will be facing the most challenging moments in their career, Christian Greiser's book comes at the right point.

Organizational change typically involves some personal "rebooting." Christian Greiser's very pragmatic approach will help any leader reflect, readjust, and rewire their own path. Super helpful, perhaps if you are planning to leave your current employer, and definitely if you want to reboot.

—ISABEL POENSGEN, Sr. Executive Coach

With a career as a top manager, BCG Senior Partner Emeritus, and Executive Coach, Christian Greiser has all the skills to enable today's executive to kick-start their engine of success. If you do not have a chance to get a coaching from him, at least read this book!

—PROF. DR. VEIT ETZOLD, best-selling author, speaker,
and managing director, Strategy & Storytelling

Christian Greiser masterfully elucidates the interplay between career highs and lows, while introducing mindfulness as a vital, yet often overlooked, resource for navigating the managerial realm. Drawing from his personal narrative, he crafts an authentic and valuable coaching approach that resonates with readers. This insightful book is a practical guide, essential for anyone embarking on their professional journey.

—BRIGITTA WURNIG, top management coach, speaker, and author

Christian has done something amazing in writing this book. He sparks the curiosity of his readers through insightful examples and stories. He illustrates the trials and tribulations of a typical career, and he does that wonderfully by taking his readers on the scenic road. You never quite know what might be behind the next curve—but you get a sense that it is something truly inspiring. He gently invites his readers to develop their own map by providing insightful examples, easy-to-understand stories, and a wealth of ideas. Written from a truly exceptional background of his own career, and with his signature humanity, this is a must-read for anyone who wants to understand their career and its potential development. Enjoy!

—ROLF PFEIFFER, managing partner, S&P Executive Advisory Partners; chair, Commonpurpose Germany

Rarely have I read a book that describes so clearly and practically how we as leaders can change our mental models, assumptions about ourselves and others, or emotional patterns in the course of our careers and life phases in order to pursue a successful career.

In the many case studies Christian Greiser describes, he shows his unusual foresight and, at the same time, precise and humorous way of guiding executives. Most of the time I was surprised by the unexpected solutions, which often prompted an "aha" response from me.

The 6 Rs, which Christian Greiser uses as a "process model," wonderfully connect the inner dimension, the inner individual processes that are sometimes our friend and sometimes our enemy, with the outer dimension, the way to the "top" in the company, providing a clear structure to reflect deeply.

—LIANE STEPHAN, co-founder and co-managing director, Awaris GmbH/Inner Green Deal gGmbH

Christian Greiser

Remove, Replace, Restart

Wir übernehmen Verantwortung! Ökologisch und sozial!

- Verzicht auf Plastik: kein Einschweißen der Bücher in Folie
- Nachhaltige Produktion: Verwendung von Papier aus
  nachhaltig bewirtschafteten Wäldern, PEFC-zertifiziert
- Stärkung des Wirtschaftsstandorts Deutschland:
  Herstellung und Druck in Deutschland

Remove, Replace, Restart

The Essential Maintenance Manual
for Your Engine for Success

Christian Greiser

External links were checked at the time the book went to print. The publisher has no control over changes that occur at a later date. Any liability of the publisher is therefore excluded.

Bibliographic information from the Deutsche Nationalbibliothek (German National Library).

The Deutsche Nationalbibliothek lists this publication in the Deutsche Nationalbibliografie (German National Bibliography); detailed bibliographic information can be accessed online at http://dnb.d-b.de.

ISBN 978-3-96739-176-3

Editing: Dr. Michael Madel, Ruppichteroth
Cover design: Guido Klütsch, Köln
Author photograph: Christian Amouzou
Composition and layout: Lohse Design, Heppenheim | www.lohsedesign.de
(German), Happenstance Type-O-Rama (English)
Translation: Hannah Campbell

Contents

MAINTENANCE MANUAL, PART II
REPLACE AND RESTART   105

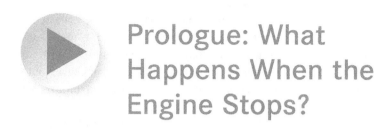

Prologue: What Happens When the Engine Stops?

*How Silence Woke Me Up from the Noise—and Turned
My Worldview Upside Down*

Ganghwa, South Korea, September 9, 2007: The Monastery

I was woken by a dull knock, as if someone were slowly hammering in a nail. It was dark, and my back was aching from the hard mattress. I fumbled, disoriented, for my watch: 3:30 a.m. Where was I? Bits and pieces of thoughts began to swirl and form a picture. *The bus journey . . . Monks . . . Monastery . . . Monastery! I'm at the monastery.* In this particular community, it was not bells that sounded the wake-up call, but the striking of hammers against wooden blocks. *Time to begin the morning ritual,* I thought. I had only a couple of minutes to get dressed. The grey meditation gown was hard and scratchy; the black fabric shoes pinched my feet. I exited my cell and met Jules, a tall Belgian man, in the corridor. "Are we going to be late?" he asked, with a touch of consternation.

"I hope not," I replied. We hurriedly made our way out of the sleeping quarters, into the darkness beyond the door, and onward to the temple on the small mound at the center of the monastery grounds. Light rain was falling.

Jules and I were guests at the monastery and had met for the first time the day before. I was in South Korea for a management consulting project. Together with my team, I'd been advising a major client—a mechanical engineering firm—on the restructuring of its Korean subsidiary. The problems were many and varied: outdated products, unprofitable prices, unproductive factories, and, inevitably, major losses. All options were on the table, including a partial relocation to China. In management consulting terms, we were dealing with a complete transformation. With an impairment review looming, we had just twelve weeks to propose a viable restructuring concept. A colleague had talked me into this adventure; I'd never even been to Korea before.

I had spent my weekends thus far in Seoul; my family was at home in Germany. Aside from a single trip back to see them, my time had been spent working or exploring South Korea's capital. I frequently found myself in Insadong, an art and antiques district filled with brush makers, seal carvers, galleries, and myriad small restaurants. The streets were colorful, lined with people, and bathed in a scent that was entirely new to me: ginseng, I was later told. I filmed short videos on my cell phone and sent them to my children. I missed my family very much.

One day, I watched a video about Zen meditation to pass time on the treadmill at the hotel gym. Here in Korea, I had learned, one could undertake a short "templestay": a weekend spent living with the monks, partaking in their daily routines and rituals, learning about Buddhist culture, sleeping under the roofs of Korea's most beautiful monasteries, and reflecting and reenergizing. I picked a weekend and signed up.

I had arrived at the monastery yesterday. The journey had been an adventure in itself: I don't speak Korean and the bus driver knew no English. Hand and foot gestures proved insufficient as a means of communication. As I floundered, assistance arrived from an unexpected source: a gaggle of giggling youths, one of whom spoke enough English to volunteer as interpreter. The bus made its way, and I was keenly questioned about where I'd come from and why I was taking the trip. When I finally disembarked in the small village near the monastery, they gazed at my surroundings with a look of distinct pity. It was as if I were heading into Dracula's castle itself.

The landscape was one of magnificent rolling hills and towering deciduous forests. As I approached the monastery, a monk greeted me with a broad smile and showed me to my room, handing me the grey clothes I'd be required to wear for my stay. I ventured outside and met the other templestayers. In addition to Jules, a sales manager at an automotive group, there were three students from France, a young Japanese medic, and an interesting older Brazilian gentleman: a former ophthalmologist who had quit the rat race and chosen to live off the grid. We sat together and chatted over a cup of tea. The remainder of the day was taken up by an introduction to the monastery's strict practices: how to enter the temple, how to bow, the meanings of the various mantras and chants. There was much to take in, yet what struck me most was the atmosphere of the place—peaceful and yet alive with energy.

A Mystical Place

I wasn't exactly sure why I had come here. Curiosity was part of it, certainly, but I was also yearning for calm. My first weeks in South Korea had been remarkably taxing. Seoul was hot and crowded. The humidity was grueling, as were the endless taxi rides through the noisy streets. The project was highly pressured, and cultural misunderstandings abounded within the team. Nobody in South Korea says no, but, as I learned, the absence of no should never be taken to mean yes. I was constantly required to read between the lines, which sapped my time and energy as the weeks went by. I had no chance to think. Here at the monastery I could switch off my cell phone and BlackBerry and get away from it all, at least for a weekend.

The others were already present as Jules and I entered the temple that morning at a jog. The space had a mystical feel: the chanting of mantras by the monks mingled with the sound of the fresh morning rain outside the open doors. The temple was lit by the atmospheric glow of candles and lanterns and scented with the aromatic smoke of incense sticks. We were led by the monks in the 108 Bows, a traditional Buddhist practice, before beginning our morning meditation. According to the brief introduction we'd been given the night before, we were to sit on the meditation cushion, channeling strength and stillness, and count our breaths from one to ten as we breathed in and out. Once we'd finished, we were to begin again. This would calm the waves of thoughts—or so the theory goes.

I found the exercise tricky that morning. Moved as I was by the spirituality of the temple, the unity of body and mind stubbornly eluded me. I was tired. My thoughts persistently wandered, and I fought hard to resist the lure of sleep. My back ached from sitting up straight on the cushion, an aftereffect, perhaps, of the hard mattress I'd slept on the night before. I felt twinges of pain in my knees. Chairs were not an option. As I looked around at Jules and the others, seated calmly on their cushions and apparently deeply relaxed, my competitive instinct began to nag at me. What was the secret to this task, anyway? All we needed to do was sit there and think about nothing. What was so hard about it? Why couldn't I do it?

Again and again I strayed into thought, never counting more than five breaths at a time. I began to agonize over my performance; in my head, it became a competitive sport. The pain in my back and knees was getting worse. I began to be consumed by a kind of internal rage. What on earth was I actually doing here? If I'd stayed in my room at the Westin Shosun hotel in Seoul, I'd still be lying in my glorious bed right now. I'd be preparing to enjoy a sumptuous continental breakfast, not the sour-smelling Korean kimchi that was served up here. Besides, I urgently needed to work on a presentation. What was I doing sitting here on the floor, surrounded by temple paraphernalia, playing at being a weekend monk? Why?! I was close to getting up and walking out in indignation.

What Remains When Everything Is Stripped Away?

As I inwardly fumed, it occurred to me suddenly that the morning rain had subsided. I listened; only a few birds could be heard beyond the temple walls. The room was blanketed in an intense silence. There was no city clamor, no cell phones, no television, no radio. It felt as though the world around me had stopped, as if somebody had pressed the pause button. At first, this brought about a deep sense of calm, and then, from nowhere, an inner voice spoke loud and clear. *Who are you now?* it said. *What are you when you're not chasing success? Who are you away from your job and family?* A part of me disappeared momentarily. I was empty, standing at the edge of an abyss, clinging on for dear life. *Let go,* continued the voice, calmly. *Take a step forward. Nothing bad is going to happen.* The intense panic that gripped me was broken only by the gong signaling the end of meditation. At once relieved and confused, I filed out of the temple with the others. *What on earth just happened?* I asked myself. *Did they put something in the incense sticks?!* I didn't mention it to the others.

The afternoon brought an invitation to a tea ceremony with the abbot of the monastery, a speaker of flawless English who possessed a calm charisma and a pleasant voice. He focused diligently on preparing the tea leaves and placing the cups on the low table. When he spoke, it was with a mixture of wit and incisiveness. He gazed at us for a long time after we'd finished our tea. "You shouldn't meditate so much," he said, his face serious. "When you stand still, you run the risk of remembering who you really are." He laughed out loud upon delivering this slice of wisdom. Perhaps it was pure coincidence, but he seemed to be looking straight at me. I sat on the floor, shocked and stock-still. *What is going on?* I thought to myself.

The ceremony over, we packed up our things and said goodbye. A monk drove us to the nearest bus stop in a rickety minibus. We had only yesterday gotten to know each other, but it felt as though it had been much longer. We didn't have long to wait: the bus to Seoul came twenty minutes later. Some of the group shared their reflections on the meditation during the journey. "I don't know if I want to stand still and remember who I really am," said Jules, laughing. "I've done pretty well without knowing so far." I stared out of the bus window and watched the green hills disappear into the distance.

Hamburg, September 11, 2021: Working from Home

I had been invited to a summer party hosted by a former consultant colleague: one of the first in-person events I'd attended since lockdown. Since everything was taking place outdoors with strict hygiene precautions, we were permitted to enjoy the evening without masks. Among the attendees, there was a tangible happiness at being able, finally, to congregate in person once more. I saw many familiar faces.

I was approached by Luca, a friend and former colleague. "Have a minute to catch up?" he asked me. We'd known each other for a number of years, having endured night shifts together on a very intensive project early in our consultancy careers. Today Luca is a partner at a private equity firm, and his long career has been a distinguished and exemplary one. That evening was our first meeting in a long time. Having chatted together with the jazz pianist who had just performed—Luca and I share the same passion for music—we were now standing companionably on the terrace, each of us with a beer in hand. We looked out onto the Elbe and admired the maritime landscape: a truly magnificent view.

What Remains When the World Stops Turning?

Luca glanced around him to make sure we wouldn't be disturbed, his face suddenly serious and contemplative. "Let's keep this between us, please," he implored me. "I want to leave the company next year. I'm not sure what I'm going to do afterward; that's something I need to think about for now. You're a coach now, aren't you? Can I get in touch for some support?"

"Any time," I said. "It'd be my pleasure. But what's the issue? Is success slower than it used to be?"

"Actually, no. Business is better than ever; we're on track for a record year."

"Oh," I said. "What's not working, then? Work/life balance?"

Luca laughed. "Oh, you know me. For sure there are times when things are hectic. We all worked more in lockdown than we ever had before. But if that were the only issue, I'd have left a long time ago."

"So, what, then?" I persisted. "Leaving without a destination? There must be a good reason for that, if it's you that's doing it."

Luca thought carefully and took a sip from his bottle of Flensburger. "Yes, I suppose you could say that. I've been thinking a lot recently, perhaps because I've found myself with more time at home. I haven't had so much quality family time in years, and work's been going pretty well. Actually, life is pretty much perfect. But, I don't know. . . . Things at work feel different than before. When lockdown happened, it was like the merry-go-round I was on just stopped. I started asking myself why I'd been doing it all—you know, the hunt for a new deal every year. I've realized that my heart's not really in it anymore. I think I'm only still doing it because I don't know any different. I don't know what comes next."

"What do you mean by the merry-go-round stopping?" I asked.

"Well, the travel, for instance," he answered. "The taxis, the flights, the conference rooms, the relentless grind. I'd never had time to think about it before. Suddenly it was all gone, and I was just sitting at home in front of a screen. Like the world had come to a standstill, and only the TV was still going."

Leaving without a Destination

"Standstill"—a notion I'd encountered often during coaching sessions in the weeks prior. There was the young manager at an automotive group who had described feeling like his engine was worn out; the IT manager experiencing her own personal system shutdown; the investment banker who found himself feeling stuck. The list was long. I would have three more conversations about it on the evening of the party alone.

Many of my clients described wanting to leave their jobs and do something completely different. Some were even prepared to quit without having a new job lined up: leaving without a destination, as it were. It seemed they were not the only ones. A recent article on the subject had talked of a "talent tsunami" and a "great resignation." It seemed as though the pandemic had changed our attitudes and brought about a shift in our priorities and values. Prior to the world shutting down, many of us lived lives in the fast lane. There was a desire to always go faster and further; a daily stream of offices, taxis, and airplanes. It was clear that these things were integral to a common understanding of success. All at once, for many of us, these glittering careers were confined to four walls and a screen. The world stood still; the news flashed surreal images of deserted airports, train stations, and streets. Success itself—or at least the many colorful manifestations of it we had come to recognize—seemed to have taken some time off. The world, spinning so fast on its axis just a moment before, had come to an emergency brake.

"It felt as though I had screeched to a halt and life was hurtling toward me from behind," a client described it. "Like a rear-end collision." Without the vibrant distractions of the world outside, it was no longer possible to escape long-neglected questions. Why are we so obsessed with chasing success? What do we mean by "success," anyway—and who are we, really, if we depend on it to define ourselves? Collectively, we had reached a standstill and been forced to think about who we were—just like I was in Korea fourteen years ago.

As many continue to ponder these uncomfortable questions, the signal to stop thinking and resume doing is being sounded ahead. Like the gong that marked the end of meditation, it tells us that the standstill is over and the world is turning once more. Back to the fast lane, back to the road to so-called success. Yet our personal engines are not cooperating. A splutter here, a creak there—something is not quite as it was before the break. There are questions we can't simply banish from our heads. We feel driven to look under the hood and to contemplate our own success more closely. What if there were a guide to doing just that?

Hamburg

"And what if you can't find the answer?" I asked Luca. "If you can't figure out where you're supposed to go, what'll you do then?"

"I've been thinking about that for weeks," he replied, "but honestly, I don't have the answer. I'm going around in circles." He paused. "But even if the pandemic is over and I still have no idea what I'm supposed to do, I think I'm going to quit anyway. This part of my life ends here; I'm sure about that."

We both looked at the Elbe for a short while longer. A huge container ship chugged past and momentarily blocked the view. We would meet in the coming weeks to talk more.

Teetering between Success and Surrender

You might say in one sense that this book is about failure. More accurately, though, it's about the moments in which personal success becomes elusive—in which we can't seem to get back to succeeding no matter what we try. It's like success has packed a bag and gone on vacation. *Be back soon, and all best wishes!* reads the imaginary postcard. How brazen! How could it take such a liberty? That wasn't what was agreed—was it?

Many a book has been written on success. In three steps, the authors promise us, we can go from student apprentice to CEO, from consultant to partner, or—in the more contemporary variant—from university dropout to millionaire entrepreneur. I've read a large number of these works. What's strange, however, is that nobody has ever mentioned them in a coaching session. *I'm currently on step number two!* the imaginary conversation might go. *I just wanted to get in touch and say that everything's going according to plan.* For some reason, that is a phone call I have yet to receive.

On the contrary: my clients often want to speak to me precisely because things *aren't* going to plan. Rather than progressing in a linear trajectory, we commonly experience unexpected hold-ups on the career highway due to misfirings of our engine for success. Such problems have become more widespread in recent years. When I look under the hood with clients, I notice broader patterns, and I fear these may be "serial errors" in the way we as humans engage with ourselves. The transition from one career phase to the next is a particularly common stumbling block; indeed, my own career has faltered at such junctures in the past. For those whose careers are already advanced, it is much too late to return to the metaphorical show-room and start again. It's time, then, for a self-help guide for those moments when success becomes elusive. It is precisely these moments that have the potential to become our most important turning points thus far.

To start, it makes sense to clarify what we mean by "success" and "career."

Success in Times of New Work and Pandemics

Shortly before completing my mechanical engineering degree in 1993, I found myself in a department store holding a book entitled *Die 100 Gesetze erfolgreicher Karriereplanung (The 100 Laws of Successful Career Planning*, Kerler and von Windau 1992). Like a book of mathematical formulas, it laid out the one hundred guiding principles one should apply in order to build a distinguished career. The systematic concept and no-nonsense structure of the book appealed to my engineer's brain, and I grabbed a copy to take home. Covering topics such as personality types, training, family, opportunities, promotion, and more, the book—in keeping with the times—presented the notion of "career" as a series of advancements in one's personal and professional circumstances. "Success" was measured by whether and how quickly such advancements took place, and its currency naturally took the form of power, prestige, and money. It was a philosophy for "yuppies" (young urban professionals), the careerists of the 1990s, for whom rapid professional advancement was the primary goal of life and whose worst excesses were embodied by characters like Gordon Gekko from the 1987 film *Wall Street*. Success was gauged by one's bank balance and business card. Thirty years have passed since then, and our understanding of success has changed radically.

My first boss ascended from the ranks of development engineer to member of the board without ever moving to a different building. His was a traditional career trajectory along a linear path. Such career paths are no more. Today, those who wish to move up professionally must forge an individual path in an ever more complex world. Those one hundred laws have evolved to become the two hundred principles of success detailed in Ray Dalio's (2019) best-selling book *Die Prinzipien des Erfolgs [Principles]*. Personal success now encompasses more than merely what we do at work and, accordingly, is measured not solely by money but by fulfillment as well. Wisdom, wonder, giving, and well-being all belong to the altogether more holistic definition of success presented in Arianna Huffington's (2014) fantastic book *Thrive*. Both Dalio and Huffington talk often of their practice of transcendental meditation, a discipline heretofore best known from the Beatles' journey to the Maharishi ashram back in the sixties. Thirty years ago, such a revelation would surely have ended the career of any top manager. Today, however, success means taking active steps to avoid burnout and to maintain a balanced life. In times of "new work"—in which freedom and self-determination are central tenets even as the boundaries between the personal and professional become increasingly blurred—physical and mental health are the new imperatives for a life successfully lived. Today, personal success is also judged by the fitness data on our smartphone apps.

Redefining Success for Times of Radical Change

Like other major historical events before it—the fall of the Berlin Wall, or the financial crises of 1929 and 2008—the COVID-19 pandemic has changed the world in lasting ways. Nowhere have these changes been more radically felt than in the world of work. Working from home was established as an alternative to the office at a breathtaking pace and on a global scale. We use videoconferencing apps like Zoom and Teams as matter-of-factly as we use an electric toothbrush. In parallel, the way we think—including and especially our understanding of success—has shifted. In this respect, the pandemic acted as a kind of catalyst, accelerating a trend that had already taken root.

We are living through a time of radical change, one that has been described as a "talent tsunami." At the beginning of 2021, a widely shared Microsoft study claimed that more than 40 percent of employees worldwide were planning a job change in the medium term (Microsoft 2021). By the end of that same year, changes in the US had borne out this gloomy business prognosis. An MIT study showed that more 24 million US Americans quit their jobs between April and September 2021, an all-time high. Innovation-focused companies—those who typically employ a large proportion of highly talented employees with above-average education levels—bore the heaviest losses. Such companies include tech firms, consultancies, and investment banks, all of which have seen dramatically increased rates of quitting over the last two years. Even prior to the pandemic, one in four start-up employees were quitting within a year (Founders Circle Capital 2022). What's going on?

Perhaps surprisingly, it's not about dissatisfaction with bonus payments or lack of promotion but about issues such as corporate culture, workload, and work/life balance. Employees are rejecting the dearth of appreciation at work, the inability to take breaks without feeling guilty for it, and the lack of opportunities to get adequate sleep or spend time with family. While from a human perspective the importance of these factors is self-evident, they have nonetheless been often neglected at the types of workplaces just described, whose oversight is now coming back to bite them. Per my conversations with start-ups, corporations, and professional services firms in Germany, the trend has also begun to establish itself there. Post-pandemic, employees' willingness to compromise quality of life and health for the sake of their careers has decreased significantly, including and especially among top talent. "Career at any cost" has had its day. Today, success is just as much predicated on one's (job-independent) sense of personal worth.

Beyond Career Planning

It goes without saying that similar trends have come and gone at times in the past. The one crucial respect in which the present economic cycle differs fundamentally from any other is that today, up to two-thirds of employees are prepared to quit without having their next job lined up (De Smet et al. 2021). As German comedian Hape Kerkeling famously titled his bestselling pilgrimage diary, *Ich bin dann mal weg* (*I'm Off Then*; Kerkeling 2006). I must admit that such a situation would have caused me sleepless nights. This, however, is due at least in part to my personality type and my generation, not to mention the absence of pandemics at any time during my active career.

It is perhaps those starting out in their careers whose perspective differs most from their counterparts in the past. In times of lockdowns, this is perfectly understandable. If one's first two years in the working world are spent in front of a screen at home, with no in-person contact with a company, jobs become as interchangeable as Netflix series. Similarly, if the next job offer is never more than a click away, the psychological barrier to a period of joblessness is reduced. (This effect is compounded in Germany by the existence of the *Erbengeneration* [generation of heirs], the cohort of individuals who, thanks to a complex combination of political and socioeconomic circumstances, are due to receive substantial individual inheritances and can thus afford to worry less about long-term financial provision. Those who have already inherited a grandparent's property have understandably fewer inhibitions about spending time without a job.)

But career starters are not the only ones. As I see time and again in my coaching, even longer-serving members of the working world are willing to countenance the idea of quitting without a firm plan. This is rooted in a change in perspective. For some, the "deal" simply no longer makes sense.

Without in-person meetings with colleagues and customers, without the Senator Lounge and business hotel, without the "VIP traveler" status satirized by many a comedian, and without fancy offices, many a dream job loses its appeal. It becomes "work hard, play hard," but without the play.

For others, the relentless mental and physical strain of lockdowns combined with endless hours at the screen has given them pause. Without real-life contact with like-minded workaholics at the office, many have—for the first time—come to appreciate the absurdity of the life they lead. The ability to work from home in close proximity to friends and family has reinforced this feeling. As it turns out, it *does* make a difference whether I, as a consultant, graft away all evening in a business hotel in New York, or whether I sit in the kitchen on a videoconference at midnight while loved ones enjoy a glass of wine next door.

Naturally, such revelations give rise to a desire to break out of the rat race and "jump off the moving train," so to speak, even if it isn't clear how soft the landing or how long the walk to the next station will be. Since the arrival of the pandemic, planning ahead has proven to be a waste of time. Why agonize and toil over a plan that may never come to fruition? Today, success also means having the freedom to take some time out.

A New Understanding of Success and Career

This mindset shift is indicative of our desire for greater self-determination with respect to what our careers look like. Today, scarcely anyone stays at one company for life. We are increasingly unwilling to allow the direction and pace of our development to be dictated by arbitrary hierarchies. Whereas in the past, promotion in itself was the benchmark for success, predefined career stages were to be checked off at any cost, and deviations from this path were regarded as career setbacks, it is gradually becoming less taboo to accumulate (ostensibly) unrelated periods of professional experience in a series of distinct career chapters. These may only become a coherent part of the narrative in retrospect and confer meaning to one's path *ex post*. Careers are sketched out freehand, not by the paint-by-numbers path of the past.

Such an approach gives rise to new career models with surprising twists and turns—and with happy endings. In a famous speech at Stanford in 2005, Steve Jobs described this approach as "connecting the dots." He is far from the only example of how great success stories can happen despite a supposedly unorthodox resume. Increasingly, unconventional job histories may even confer an advantage. Take a former colleague of mine who quit an established career, founded a start-up, sold it successfully, and then spent a year caring for his family before joining the board at a major retail group. Many candidates with a "model resume" may wait forever for such an offer to come their way. Careers today are different. Personal success is predicated on development and fulfillment—and this includes time out from the mainstream rat race.

When Success Turns to a Standstill

An experienced coach and trainer once told me that "your development as a leader occurs in three stages." He was referring to a model of leadership popularized by energy giant GE, among others (Charan, Drotter, and Noel 2001). "You first learn to lead yourself, then to lead others, and finally to lead your organization. Which of these do you think is most important?" I thought of how challenging it must be to lead a large organization and all its many members. "The third," I answered.

"It's the first," he said. "To be able to lead, you must first understand who you are and who you are not. Some people spend their whole lives trying and failing to figure this out, even when they already hold important leadership roles."

It's not for nothing that the words "Know thyself" are inscribed above the entrance to the temple of Apollo at Delphi. It could be argued that they are even more relevant now than they were two millennia ago. If personal success is to be defined in terms of fulfillment, self-development, and self-actualization—and if, on this basis, we are to embrace greater responsibility for our own professional development—it is critical to understand who we are and who we are not. Whether we wish to launch our own e-car start-up à la Elon Musk or to simply progress better as an employee in a corporate setting, there can be no getting away from the importance of personality type. If we, too, are to "find our thing" and achieve something approaching professional fulfillment, it is vital that we first reflect honestly on a number of things: what gets us out of bed in the morning, which skills and tasks we have mastered to perfection, which we would rather avoid, when we need to give ourselves a kick in the pants, and how we know when we need to take a break. In short: to be able to lead ourselves, we need to get to know ourselves better. We must also understand that this learning process is not linear, but rather progresses in cycles.

The "Performance Curve" of Our Personal Engine for Success

We enter the working world with a plethora of ambitions, hopes, fears, and illusions, yet with relatively little knowledge about ourselves. There is no manual to refer to when things go awry; rather, we must develop our own set of guiding principles over time. As we progress through each rung of a professional career, we gain expertise and experience in a particular field, but we also learn what our talents are, what motivates us, what is important to us, and, just as crucially, what we are not so good at. This learning process is often visualized in the form of an S-curve, as can be seen in the book *Disrupt Yourself* by Whitney Johnson (2019) as well as in the aforementioned *Die 100 Gesetze erfolgreicher Karriereplanung* (Kerler and von Windau 1992) from some thirty years prior. Our career progression follows the same curve, since logically, the degree to which we amass expertise and learn about ourselves also determines the extent of our success.

The first portion of the curve is flat. In this phase, we are finding our feet in a new professional environment. We learn slowly and are correspondingly slow to achieve success. After some time, we reach what has been described as the "tipping point" (Gladwell 2001), which represents a breakthrough, the start of a new phase in which we have fully understood how our job works and discovered new talents and strengths. Our personal "engine for success" gears up to full capacity, the curve moves steeply upward, and—typically—we experience a high degree of personal fulfillment. Sometime later, we reach a turning point, after which the learning curve slowly plateaus, a sense of routine creeps in, and we may begin to feel occasionally stifled or bored. This phase continues until we reach the apex. After this, success stagnates, each day feels the same as the one before, and our job ceases to be "fun." This is the time for the next rung of the ladder and the next career cycle to begin. With each passing cycle, our baseline level of knowledge increases and we learn more and more about ourselves. It is by passing through several of these cycles in succession, perhaps with the occasional break in between, that we achieve a fulfilled professional life.

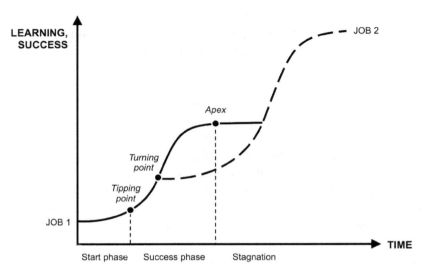

The career cycle

The progression of the S-curve also reveals how our personal engine for success functions in each of the previously described phases. Consider the analogy of driving a car. When we move from one rung of the career ladder to the next, it is important that we don't attempt to engage the next gear forcefully without bothering to use the clutch. Similarly, we must not attempt to force the car from the first gear directly into the fourth. Either of these courses of action would risk stalling the engine. Instead, we must ease our way through the phases smoothly and gradually, shifting up and down through the gears one by one. In practice, this means mentally initiating the change not at the apex, but at the turning point: when things are still progressing satisfactorily, but we feel intuitively that we will soon be ready for the next challenge. It is at this point that we have sufficient energy and motivation to think productively about the future—and sufficient time to prepare thoroughly and ensure that we're qualified for the next phase. By taking this approach, we can succeed in moving up the gears without unwelcome thuds and clunks. Indeed, we see such an approach adopted at the very top levels of management, where successor candidates for a CEO position "warm up" for a year or more before taking over the top job. We now have an idea of the theory and best practice. In the real world, of course, bumps in the road are commonplace, and I recognize these as much from my clients as from my own experience in the corporate world.

When the Engine Stutters

I'll preface this section by saying that in regard to my own life, I have very little grounds for complaint. My professional trajectory has mostly progressed without complications; for great distances, the engine powering my own career has passed smoothly through the cycles just described. Still, though, there are certain times and places in which it has ground to an unexpected and unwelcome halt. My trusted formulas for success ceased to bring the results I was used to, and business did not go as hoped. I was beset by a feeling that I was failing to fulfill the expectations placed upon me, and as a result, I worked longer, harder, and with greater self-pressure than before. Whatever I tried, my previous success seemed to elude me. My engine stuttered and I was stuck, immobile, on the success curve. This happened most often after big career jumps: periods when I was trying to move up through the metaphorical gears. It was at these times that I had to shake things up internally and get the engine going again, hoping I had not burnt it out.

There were other defining moments, too—moments in which things were going ostensibly well and in which, by all accounts, I should have felt satisfied, if only I didn't have the nagging sense that I was moving in the wrong direction. At the time, these moments also felt like precursors to a standstill of success. I later realized that this initial assessment was mistaken. The longer I thought about it, the clearer it became that, actually, my personal definition of success was evolving. My values had shifted; the relative importance of things in my life had changed. Mathematically speaking, you could say that the axes of the S-curve had been redefined. Instead of approaching a new point on the old curve, I found myself on a completely different graph. What had felt like the start of a plateau had in fact been a new beginning.

Looking back, I can identify two distinct triggers for these shifts. The first of these was radical experiences; the second, the opportunity to devote significant time to introspection and reflection. "When the mind is quiet," a Zen master once told me, "the truth of the world will reveal itself." "Unexpected behavior," a mechanic would say. What does this mean in regard to our engine use?

A Look under the Hood

In the course of conducting "under the hood" explorations with my coaching clients, I came to a realization. Many of them were complaining of the same problems I had once faced myself: their engines for success were stuttering at the same familiar junctures. Clear patterns were observable. *Aha!* I thought. These cases weren't a question of improper engine use per se, but of "serial errors" in us as humans. Upon further examination, I identified six main reasons for the career-stalling engine issues I was encountering repeatedly in these exchanges:

Reason 1: The inability to manage our own resources
Reason 2: Blind spots and an unawareness of our own driving forces
Reason 3: The inability to let go of old models of success
Reason 4: Difficulty adopting new habits
Reason 5: A lack of courage to reinvent ourselves in line with the times
Reason 6: Naivete in tackling a career restart

Reason 1: The Inability to Manage Our Own Resources

When an engine is run at top speed for a long time, it becomes hot. Sooner or later, it gives up completely. The relevance of this analogy for us is clear. Those who want to avoid burning out by age thirty must treat their own resources with prudence and care. It is an unfortunate fact of life that we frequently overestimate ourselves. We drive long stretches with our foot to the floor, neglecting to take breaks or pay heed to the warning lights. It's little wonder, then, that the engine burns out when we least expect it.

Reason 2: Blind Spots and an Unawareness of Our Own Driving Forces

There are two stories told about any given one of us: the one we tell about ourselves and the one devised by others. Insofar as we have a means of obtaining honest feedback and are willing to accept it, we are able to reconcile the two stories, eliminate blind spots, and acquire new knowledge. If we do not, we run the risk of failure; worse still, of being unable to understand why we have failed. By the same token, there will always be situations in which we struggle to implement such feedback. In these cases, we must delve deeper into the "engine compartment" to recognize the covert driving forces that motivate us. There, more often than not, lies the root of the problem. Without this knowledge, we might as well be fighting a ghost.

Reason 3: The Inability to Let Go of Old Models of Success

Success can render us blind. When we are successful, we move up the career ladder. It stands to reason, then, that we continue to do what got us there and to remain faithful to our existing principles. The problem is that when we do this, we risk becoming presumptuous and resistant to criticism, adopting a veneer of infallibility based on our previous success. Eventually, like Icarus flying too close to the sun, we fall out of the sky and meet an unenviable end. To avoid such pitfalls and remain truly open to new ideas, we must ask questions of ourselves in each new phase of our career and be prepared to leave behind the habits and principles that got us there. If this seems paradoxical, it's because it is—and it's not easy to accept or to implement.

Reason 4: Difficulty Adopting New Habits

Just as we replace worn or broken parts in a car, we must acquire new skills and habits from time to time. The old ones have simply run their course, and it is incumbent upon us to evolve accordingly. This isn't so easy, however, because good intentions alone won't suffice. When we attempt to rely on willpower, we're likely to fall into a familiar trap: we resolve to do something with the best of intentions—to reach out to customers more often, for example—only to keep it up for two weeks before becoming mired in a sea of excuses. Before long, the good intention is forgotten. To establish and maintain new habits, we must secure them just as we tighten lug nuts after changing a tire; otherwise, they'll simply fall off again.

Reason 5: A Lack of Courage to Reinvent Ourselves in Line with the Times

Hard work leads to success in equal measure. Or does it? Our brain loves systems that behave in a linear fashion, those in which cause and effect are directly correlated. When things become more nuanced, we struggle—as the S-shaped success curve succinctly shows. When the curve is rising steeply, it is difficult for us to accept in earnest that a plateau is just around the corner. *Is it really necessary to trouble ourselves with thoughts of the future right now, when everything is going so well?* we ask. *Who knows: maybe next year will be even better!* Granted, we may occasionally experience nagging feelings of internal emptiness, but to proactively reinvent ourselves? That would be the far greater of two evils. *After all, the job is still a good fit; even our families, friends, and colleagues think so.* So great is our ability to dither and procrastinate that we inadvertently sail past our own sell-by date.

Reason 6: Naivete in Tackling a Career Restart

Sometimes success is put on pause because we're taking a break from work itself. Perhaps we have elected to take a sabbatical or, unfortunately, lost a job. Perhaps we have reached the third phase of life—the end of "regular" work—and are taking a break before starting again with something new. Finding our way back to the road to success can require an effort that shouldn't be underestimated. The inevitable truth is that the world will have continued to turn in our absence: it is only our engine that has stood still. Our task now is to restart the flywheel, and that can require us to push harder than we think.

A Maintenance Manual to Keep Us on the Road

What are we to do when success turns to a standstill? The answer, simply put, is to let go of precisely those things that made us successful in the past. We must stop carelessly maxing out our resources. We must admit we do not know ourselves half as well as we think. We must surrender old formulas for success: they've had their time and should be laid to rest. We must let go of the belief that willpower can achieve anything: if we are honest with ourselves, this has never really worked. We must say goodbye to our established professional identity: it's last year's model in last year's clothes. We must detach ourselves from the belief that the world cannot do without us: it's more than a little arrogant, and untrue to boot. *Okay*, you might be thinking, *and how do I achieve all this?* To illustrate that, I'd like to tell you a story.

A Trip to the Countryside

Imagine, for a moment, that you're in your car heading to a picnic on a hot summer morning. The day looks promising; then, out of nowhere, the engine begins to stutter and a warning light comes on. You *reduce your speed*, come to a stop, keep a clear head, and open the hood. You wonder if the noises are the problem or just the symptom: *resolving* the question of cause and effect is not so easy. Unfortunately, it turns out, the car must be towed away. The picnic will not happen, at least not today.

At the mechanic's shop, the old, long-used-up oil is *removed* by draining. Unfortunately, there are also worn parts to be *replaced*. Such problems have cropped up repeatedly in recent months. You toy with the idea of a new car and *rigorously test* a range of models in the coming weeks. You like one model much more than the rest—but is it really the change you need? You hesitate. The decision requires time. Then, a spanner in the works: the old car finally gives up the ghost. Annoyed, you decide to simply live without one.

For almost a year, things are good. Then doubts begin to creep in: is something missing? Life without a car is so impractical, after all. You decide on a new car, but as you sit at the wheel and *restart* your life as a vehicle owner, you realize to your surprise that it will take some getting used to again. It's not just you that needs a little practice—the new car also requires "breaking in." Finally, though, you and your new steed find yourselves in harmony. You head through the countryside to the picnic at last. All problems are forgotten. A happy ending!

But what does this have to do with your job and your success? You might be surprised to realize that when career problems occur, the course is very similar. When your engine for success stutters, you can apply the steps (the six Rs) from the preceding story:

- **Reduce speed:** Recognize and respond to warnings.
- **Resolve:** Untangle cause and effect.
- **Remove:** Discard patterns of behavior that no longer benefit you.
- **Replace:** Adopt new ways of doing things.
- **Rigorously test:** Experiment with new identities.
- **Restart:** Regain momentum after a break.

This is precisely what this book is about. My wish is that, like a maintenance manual, it will help you troubleshoot the problem and get back on the road to where you want to be. Whenever your personal engine stutters, think of the trip to the countryside. You'll realize you already know the right thing to do.

How to Use This Book

I want to provide this book with a little "instruction page" of its own. It is based on practical experience and written for practical use. It is aimed at people who find themselves at a professional turning point—where things seem not to be moving forward—and who feel the time is right to take the next step on their personal development path.

This could include those who have already made the formal leap to the board, the executive team, or the partner role of a professional services firm, but have yet to adjust their mindset accordingly. The book should also appeal to those who are on their way to the top: those who have taken on leadership responsibility for the first time and are learning a lot about themselves in the process. It might also be of interest to entrepreneurs who have set their company on the desired growth path, but are experiencing self-doubt and a feeling of having reached their personal limits.

This book is for leaders and managers who would approach a coaching session with questions and a search for clarity. If this is you, I am confident the book will provide at least the initial answers.

I have chosen to illustrate my approach with a car-based analogy. This is not because I wanted to aim the book primarily at male readers; it is, of course, merely a stereotype that men "appreciate" cars more anyway. The book is for men and women equally. Moreover, my use of this analogy is in no way intended to express support for the combustion engine. On the contrary: I simply considered it fitting, knowing that most of us still drive (or have driven) combustion engine cars and are familiar with the problems they can bring. This, after all, is the reason for using an analogy at all: to make abstract concepts tangible and thus better understandable. That was the engineer side of me coming through.

The book is, as discussed, intended as a kind of maintenance manual. It doesn't claim to be a scientific treatise. It is based on experience gathered during my own career and my work as a coach, and contains tried-and-tested concepts that have proven themselves in practice for the challenges at hand. Where appropriate, I have added research to support the effectiveness of the methods and tools. Note, though, that I make no claim to the completeness of my theses; on the contrary, I would be delighted to receive further input from readers to help shed light on other common career stoppers.

Finally, a note on confidentiality. My wish was to write an engaging, practice-oriented book with real-life examples and case studies. The decision to use many examples from my own career was partially to eliminate the confidentiality issue: I could decide for myself what to disclose and what not to disclose. For my clients, it is different. In order to maintain confidentiality, I have amended names, events, and details so that none of the individuals can be personally identified. I hope that many readers of this book will identify with and recognize themselves in the characters and situations portrayed.

Happy reading!

MAINTENANCE MANUAL, PART I

RECOGNIZE AND RESPOND

Why Old Formulas for Success Suddenly
Cease to Function . . .
and Why Questions Then Become
More Important Than Answers

Reduce Speed: Recognizing and Responding to Warning Signs

If a warning light suddenly comes on—even a seemingly innocuous one—your alarm bells should start ringing. If it is safe to do so, stop your vehicle immediately and switch off the engine.
—MOTORISTS' ADVICE WEBSITE AUTOFAHRERSEITE.EU, 2022

On one occasion or another, many of us will deal with an unexpected warning light while driving. *Something's wrong with the engine,* we might think. Of course, we don't continue to press on the gas; we pull over immediately and stop the car. Our approach to our professional lives should be no different. Indeed, a failure to do so—in other words, a lack of ability to manage our own resources—represents the first career stopper from the list in the previous chapter. When our inner warning light begins to glow, our first action should be to shift down the gears, come to a stop, and keep a cool head. A little distance affords perspective and a more incisive assessment of the situation. To illustrate this, here is Sarah's story.

Case Study: Sarah

It's a clear Friday morning in October. I meet Sarah in her office, a modern room with windows offering expansive views over the manufacturing site. Sarah is responsible for the quality department at a major manufacturer of specialist machinery.

The Background

Sarah studied mechanical engineering and graduated summa cum laude. Now in her early thirties, she has been at the company for five years and hasn't always found it easy to assert herself in the male-dominated corporate culture. For her, the challenge isn't an unfamiliar one: it's something she remembers well from her studies. At university, Sarah pursued her academic interests and consciously decided on a technical discipline. It runs in the family—her father was also an engineer.

Sarah is the ideal fit for the quality department. Not only are her analytical skills extremely strong, but her colleagues praise her almost magical ability to troubleshoot the causes of problems. Her tenure at the company has been exemplary, and she has now been responsible for quality globally for two years. It's difficult to arrange an appointment with her; her calendar is hopelessly overcrowded. Today is our second coaching session.

The Session Begins

"I must apologize," she says, after we've greeted each other. "Today's really not my day—I barely got any sleep last night. The problems seem to be never-ending. To be honest, I'd even thought about postponing this session again, but I knew if I did that it wouldn't happen at all."

"What's going on?" I ask with interest.

"A mechanical breakdown on a construction site. We don't know why. Obviously, everyone's looking at me—and so they should. Things like that shouldn't happen with our quality standards. I've been working day and night to try to resolve it."

"It sounds like you haven't had time for much else."

"No, I haven't," she replies. "It's really testing my expectations of myself and my department. We keep having issues with the new machine series and we still don't know the cause of the problem. Half the company's talking about it. I can't shake the feeling that some of my colleagues in management have written me off when it comes to solving it."

"Have your colleagues said as much?" I ask.

"No," she replies, "but I can see it in their faces."

"Okay," I reply, "so that's what you think you're seeing. And what are you hearing?"

"I talk to the HR director regularly," she says. "She's my mentor. She always stresses how much everyone supposedly appreciates me. She sees me as the 'only one who's across all these issues.'"

"But that should reassure you," I counter.

"I think perhaps she's just saying it to pacify me," she answers, "and I'm going to end up paying for everything sooner or later. It's set off an alarm signal; something isn't quite right anymore."

"How do you mean?"

"It's strange. Sometimes I believe in myself and I feel sure I can manage everything. Other times, I feel I'm not the right person for the job at all. I've started trusting myself less and less, and I'm pushing myself harder as a result. Work's starting to take over my life."

"Interesting," I say. "It sounds like you're talking about two separate people: one who works diligently for all hours of the day, and another who berates the first one with predictions of failure and negative comparisons with others. In other words, you're not exactly being easy on yourself."

"To be honest, sometimes I do feel like there are two different people inside me," she answers thoughtfully.

"If the warning light is already on, you should think about taking things down a gear," I say. "Otherwise, before you know it, you'll have made the damage worse. And this isn't a machine we're talking about–it's your health. How many breaks do you take in a day?"

"I can't take breaks at the moment," she replies wearily. "Where would I find the time? We're in a state of emergency!"

The Vital Importance of Time for Ourselves

We go to Sarah's computer and look at her calendar: a patchwork quilt of one appointment after the next. Her days appear to consist solely of meetings. She doesn't have even half an hour to herself.

"Let's forget the day-to-day stuff for a moment," I say. "How do you see your life in ten years' time?"

Sarah thinks for a moment. "I'm successful at my job. I have a family, I enjoy a social life outside of work, and I have time to be spontaneous again." As she says this, she suddenly seems much more alive.

"Try to be a bit more specific," I tell her.

"I've helped to build something completely new at work. I have children. I'm part of a network that promotes women in technical professions, and . . ." She pauses to think. "And I've learned to surf. I've always loved the sea and the waves. With all the waves we have to ride here, learning to surf might not be a bad thing," she says, laughing.

"Fantastic. And where do these dreams feature in your life at present?"

"As good as nowhere at all," she replies wistfully.

"You need a strategy for yourself, then," I reply, "or your batteries will be drained before you know it. For a start, how about scheduling two hours of time for yourself every week? I recommend you use it for personal reflection and for turning your dreams into concrete goals—ones you can work on and make space for in your calendar. At the same time, you should try to get a little more sleep. How does that sound?"

The First Steps

We work on Sarah's weekly schedule in the following weeks. She begins to prioritize things differently, focusing on strategically important tasks and on herself. She no longer attends every meeting; she delegates much more and learns to say no. She takes regular breaks at work, resumes her morning yoga sessions (a practice from her student days), and plans weekly "time out" to work on her personal strategy. She and a friend arrange to call each other and keep each other accountable for taking breaks. Bit by bit, Sarah begins to get her energy back.

The Breakthrough

One Friday evening a few weeks later, my telephone rings. "I hope I'm not interrupting your weekend," Sarah says, "but I need to speak to you for a moment, please."

"Any time," I reply.

"I knew it from the start. I should have trusted my gut instinct."

"What's this about?" I ask with interest.

"We've found the fault in the new machine series. It's the housing. We used a welded construction, because we couldn't get the cast parts from Eastern Europe anymore. This was causing vibration issues when the machines were started up. I had a hunch the whole time, but I'd gotten so bogged down in the details that I couldn't see the forest for the trees. I'd stopped trusting my gut. I could have saved us a lot of time and hassle. But anyway, it's solved now."

"Congratulations! Maybe you really do have magical powers, like your colleagues say," I laugh.

"Thank you. But that's not the reason I'm calling on a Friday evening. Unfortunately, I need to cancel our coaching session next week. I'm sorry about the short notice."

"A new mechanical problem?" I ask.

"No. I'm treating myself to a little something. I've taken a few days' vacation, and . . ." She falters briefly.

"And what?" I ask, interested.

"You won't believe it, but I'm learning to kitesurf. I signed up for a course on the spur of the moment. I can't wait. Nothing will be able to blow me down after that!" I can hear her smiling.

"I'm already looking forward to hearing about it," I assure her. Our next coaching session is in three weeks' time.

What We Can Learn from Sarah

▶ *Stay attentive; don't be seduced by success.*

Sarah's talent and will to succeed earned her an important management position early on in her career. But because she defined herself solely by professional success, this personal crisis was inevitable sooner or later. The moment success began to elude her, her self-image crumbled. She blamed herself entirely for what had gone wrong. Sarah fits the mold of a classic "insecure overachiever": everyone believes in her except for herself. In this example, Sarah had stopped trusting herself and, in so doing, had lost the asset of her intuition. Her natural inclination to push herself to her personal limits, combined with her inability to say no, had almost caused her burnout.

▶ *Listen to your inner alarm bells.*

Sarah sensed that something was no longer right: an inner warning light had come on. Happily for her, she took this warning seriously. By making space for her long-term hopes and dreams, Sarah found a way out of the mental fight-or-flight mode of the daily grind and put herself in a positive frame of mind. Only then was she able to recognize that she'd been going the wrong way the whole time. It was time, she realized, for a course correction. Engaging mentally with her long-term goals replenished the energy and motivation she needed.

▶ *Most importantly, manage your energy and allow time off.*

Sarah's calendar was hopelessly overcrowded because she dedicated her life solely to meeting her own and others' high expectations. Accordingly, she initially defined her problem as one of "not enough time." In reality, however, she had an energy problem. Her reserves were almost exhausted. In order to recognize this, she needed to get some distance from the situation and learn to say no. By taking regular breaks to recharge her batteries and getting back in touch with her body through yoga, she restored her energy and intuition and, as a result, her problem-solving abilities. She used a friend's support to good effect to firmly embed her resolutions. The fact that Sarah rewarded herself for her progress with a kitesurfing course and avoided falling back into her old habits shows that her changes were not merely token efforts; rather, her entire perspective had begun to shift.

Keep reading to the end of this chapter to find out what happened to Sarah next.

On Alarm Signals, Time Out, and Attentiveness

Leaders must be able to lead themselves. They must be able to read and interpret their own feelings in order to recognize inner alarm signals before it's too late. They must manage their resources effectively and allow themselves downtime—not only once or twice, but as often as they need it. Instead of getting swept away by trains of negative thought, they must be able to observe these thoughts and bring them (back) under control as needed. This is what the following section is about.

Alarm Signals: Why It Pays to Listen to How We Feel

"We've come a long way in terms of sustainability and digitalization. Two years ago, no one would have thought that we'd be here. Our accounts are healthier than ever; customers are beating down our doors. And now we've had to suspend all deliveries because we can't get materials and half the workforce is out with COVID. Should I laugh or cry? I mean, seriously, can you imagine what I'm feeling right now?" This is how one board member described the emotional ups and downs that are so characteristic of modern business. He is no exception. Perhaps you've felt like this, too.

Wanted: Leaders with Emotional Superpowers

Today's leaders face increasing challenges. We are experiencing concurrent waves of ecological, technological, societal, and geopolitical change at an intensity never before seen. Sustainability is now at the top of the CEO agenda, the COVID crisis has turned our working world upside down, digitalization and artificial intelligence are revolutionizing corporate processes, millennials are driving cultural change in organizations, and the Ukraine war is creating drastic supply bottlenecks and pressing questions about business location.

If managers wish to succeed in the face of these challenges, they can't be easily rattled. They must have a stable inner self and know themselves inside out. They must be able to assess situations rationally and maintain emotional balance instead of oscillating between euphoria and doom. They must be calm and confident, concentrate on the here and now, and master the stormy waves with the skill of a champion surfer. They must be capable of addressing their own feelings and those of others in a productive manner. In short, leaders with emotional superpowers are now very much in demand.

How Emotional Intelligence Can Make or Break a Career

The skill of emotional intelligence, in particular, is increasingly important as we move up the career ladder. *Emotional intelligence* is our ability to identify our own and others' feelings, to understand them and to deal with them in an appropriate manner. The concept of emotional intelligence was popularized by Daniel Goleman in his best-selling book of the same name (Goleman 1997), which proposed an emotional intelligence framework comprising five domains: self-awareness, self-regulation, motivation, empathy, and social skills (Goleman 2022). Although feelings are still rarely discussed in the boardroom, where analytics and logic are the foundation of day-to-day business, emotional intelligence as a concept has begun to filter through to the upper echelons of corporate management. Generally speaking, in my experience, many managers score high on domains such as motivation and social skills; after all, they tend to have energy and stamina and the learned ability to build and maintain networks. When it comes to empathy, self-awareness, and self-regulation, however, they often have a good deal of room for improvement.

Empathy

Anyone who wishes to succeed at the top levels of modern management requires more than purely professional skills, especially when it comes to initiating and leading major transformations. *Empathy*—the ability to understand the feelings of others—is as vital as any technical expertise. Without empathy, an individual will find it almost impossible to engender the desired motivation and spirit of optimism within a leadership team, let alone to inspire young talent. The problem, as a board member once told me, is that those who have long defined themselves solely by their analytical prowess may find it difficult to switch to empathy mode. They struggle to embrace this fashionable "soft skill."

Self-Awareness

Those who wish to understand the feelings of others must first come to grips with their own emotional world. This requires *self-awareness*: the ability to recognize one's own moods, values, goals, preferences, drives, and feelings and to understand how they influence one's behavior. The goal is *not* to reach a place where we no longer feel stressed by an overcrowded calendar, but instead to identify the reasons for stress being present in the first place. For a variety of reasons, some leaders lose the ability to perceive and acknowledge their own feelings. This, in my view, is a fundamental problem with wide-reaching effects.

Self-Regulation

If self-awareness means recognizing our feelings, *self-regulation* is what enables us to control them. It is the ability to avoid rash decisions and judgments and not be swept away on a torrent of emotion. I often speak to leaders who have fallen into this trap and have later come to regret an emotional outburst. I once took part in a steering group in which the furious CEO publicly sacked his production manager, only to apologize to him afterward and ask him to stay. "I was a bit emotional," as he put it.

Emotional intelligence is an ever more vital tool for modern leaders. While research shows that it can, to a certain extent, be learned and trained, this presupposes that all who would benefit from such training are able to recognize their deficit in the first place. This, in turn, requires the ability to self-reflect. The problem is that some managers find this difficult. They are adept neither at recognizing and understanding their own feelings nor at bringing them under control. This problem is also linked to their self-image.

SOS: A Distress Call from Our Emotional Center

Those who hitch their self-esteem too strongly to their external success find themselves adrift on oscillating waves of emotion every time they face an external obstacle. They are like lifeboats without rudders, buffeted around mercilessly by their emotions and bouncing back and forth between euphoria and dejection. This cycle of ups and downs makes it increasingly difficult for them to assess and manage situations rationally. Their self-confidence falls with every failure. At some point, they begin to panic at what they perceive as a career in serious jeopardy. They push harder and work more. It is at this point that a warning light should come on—unless, of course, they've already pulled the plug on the system.

"I have to step on the gas now, get the horsepower on the road," a young investment manager told me. "Otherwise, I can forget about promotion." Fatigue and exhaustion were etched on his face, but he didn't seem to feel it. His warning light had apparently failed. It is a mindset I recognize all too well: for a long time, I, too, considered seventy-plus-hour workweeks to be "normal." If a warning light threatened to derail my progress, I knew just how to pull the plug. I learned to detach myself from my pain and feelings, just as one is taught to do in martial arts. In psychology, this concept is known as *dissociation*. It is dangerous. Disconnecting the temperature probe does nothing to keep the engine cool: it simply means we're no longer aware if and when it is running hot. Sooner or later, engine damage is inevitable.

As I know from personal experience, emotions aren't always easy to deal with. They must be correctly identified in the first instance, and this in itself can be an unwelcome challenge.

The ABCs of Emotions

"Yes, time to celebrate!" "Grrr, I was robbed!" There are moments in business in which the associated emotions are easy to identify: joy and pride at bonus time, or anger and frustration after a missed promotion. Sometimes we have only a vague feeling that something is amiss: a nonspecific anxiety triggered by the pressure to succeed in a new role, for example. In these situations, it's important to listen to ourselves and get to the bottom of things.

How many emotions can humans actually feel? Psychologist Paul Ekman distinguishes between seven basic emotions: sadness, anger, surprise, fear, disgust, contempt, and happiness (Ekman 2010). Each encompasses a subgroup of related emotions. Note, however, that "negative" emotions, such as fear, don't necessarily have to be perceived as unpleasant; for example, many people relish the brief experience of fear from a rollercoaster at an amusement park. Being able to pinpoint our emotions takes some practice. The following exercise can help you calibrate your inner emotional probe and warning lights correctly.

Exercise: Getting to Know Your Feelings Better

- Over the coming week, make a note of how you feel three times per day (for example, morning, noon, and evening). Write down how strongly you feel the feeling on a scale from 1 (a little) to 10 (a lot).
  Is the feeling hazy or clear? Can you put a name to it? Also make a note of what you're doing at the time. Feel free to use either a paper diary or a modern mood tracker app such as Daylio (https://daylio.net/), MoodPanda (https://moodpanda.com/), or iMoodJournal (https://www.imoodjournal.com/).
- Review the results at the end of the week. What do you notice? Which feelings did you experience particularly frequently? Which feelings did you not experience at all?

Great Things Happen When the Gut and Head Work in Harmony

When it comes to recognizing and understanding our feelings, each of us has a valuable ally at our disposal in the form of our own body. Our body gives physiological signals as soon as it senses an inner warning light. This is why it's important to listen to and trust it.

Research by neuroscientist Antonio R. Damasio shows that the relationship between emotions and bodily signals is indispensable for our survival. He describes somatic markers that unconsciously guide us to one decision or another based on how our body feels (Damasio 2004). We know this as a *gut feeling* or *intuition*: a scientifically proven phenomenon that has nothing to do with esotericism. Intuition is also important in higher management, never more so than when the facts are on the table and must somehow be translated into the right strategic decision. Former PepsiCo CEO Indra K. Nooyi describes intuition as the ability to "look around the corner and connect the dots into lines and shapes where others might not see them" (Ensser 2014).

When making gut decisions, the brain falls back on its memory of experience: the part of the brain that stores knowledge in the form of emotional and somatic responses to past events. This is used to make simple snap judgments, such as "good: approach" or "bad: avoid." These signals, triggered in the blink of an eye, are vague and nonspecific, which is why gut feelings are usually difficult to describe. They are worth trusting, though, because they often help us to make the correct decision. A surfer, for example, has only a fraction of a second to decide their next move and must be guided by the way their body feels in the moment. Similarly, a strategist must rely on gut feelings when making a "blue ocean decision" to establish a new market. When we feel intuitively that we should shut the laptop and get some sleep, we can count on the fact that our body knows what's best for us.

Those who have sharp analytical minds but are not adept at perceiving their own bodily signals often miss vital information. The character of Sheldon Cooper in the US television series *The Big Bang Theory* is a comedic portrayal of such a personality type. Because such people struggle to access intuition as a means of confirming their decisions, they rely solely on external factors to verify the correct path. In stressful situations, their inner warning light may be flashing as violently as the beacon on a fire truck, but they themselves don't perceive this. Their input comes solely from their rational mind, which tells them: "Go on, try harder; you can figure it out." For these individuals, the ability to perceive bodily signals must be trained. Instead of reading their third book of the week, it would be preferable to take a yoga class or learn to kitesurf, like Sarah from our case study. This is what I recommend to my clients. It makes our body happy when we consciously inhabit it—and we make the best decisions when we listen to both our mind *and* our gut feelings, when gut and head are working in harmony.

Once we learn to perceive what we are feeling, we can also sense when an inner warning light comes on. We have regained control over ourselves.

Time Out: How We Can Get the Most Out of Our Personal Resources

We're all likely familiar by now with Earth Overshoot Day: the point in each calendar year when we as a society have consumed more ecological resources than can be replenished in 365 days. Our personal resources work in a similar way. When our inner warning light flickers on—if not beforehand—we must consciously shift down a gear to ensure that we don't burn through our resources faster than we can build them back up. Unlike the planet, we hold the power to determine whether or not to make this choice. Despite having this important tool at our disposal, we often proceed as if our powers were limitless, like a hero or heroine from a Marvel comic. This is misguided.

Space, the Final Frontier. The Year Is 2022 . . .

It always makes me smile to see how old science fiction series imagined the future. Almost fifty years ago, "Kirk to *Enterprise*" was the famous refrain spoken by Captain Kirk into his now-iconic "communicator"—a small device that looked like a modest predecessor of our smartphone—in the television series *Star Trek*. The world we have ended up in looks slightly different. Today, the opening credits to the legendary series might go something like: "These are the voyages of the Starship *Enterprise*, its five-year mission . . . to explore strange new worlds . . . to boldly go where no man has gone before. Of course, the *Enterprise* crew is always on, always connected, always reachable: twenty-four hours a day, seven days a week, via WhatsApp, Zoom, or Teams. Their smartphones, iPads, and MacBooks are by their sides on every new adventure."

Welcome to the future. Today's gadgets and apps allow us to communicate in real time with friends, colleagues, or customers from New York to Tokyo and to work from anywhere in the world. Captain Kirk would be thrilled! Digital possibilities were our savior in the COVID crisis, yet they also come at a cost. Boundaries between the personal and professional are becoming increasingly blurred; we are less and less able to stop and switch off. "It's easy to find the button to close the app," a client of mine put it, "it's just hard to actually press it." Our work/life balance begins to tip in the wrong direction and to deplete our physical reserves. Where is the lever to move things down a gear?

Caution! Please Step Back: Your Life Is Arriving

"I already know I need to move down a gear," says Lynn, a stressed and overworked investment banker. "And I've got an idea, too. I want to run a marathon next year, and I'm going to take time to prepare properly. I've set myself an ambitious target: I want to get well under the four-hour mark." Lynn makes an all-too-common mistake: she believes she's moved into the "breakdown lane," but she's still firmly stuck in a "fast lane" mindset. Shifting down a gear means recharging your batteries and creating mental space to work on yourself. It also means getting distance from your current situation in order to be able to recognize your problems at all.

When we want to appreciate a van Gogh painting, we don't stand with our nose directly to the canvas, but take a step back for a broader view. Gaining perspective on our problems requires the same approach. When it comes to figuring out what's going wrong in our life and how to make it better, it's not realistic to expect to arrive at conclusions in the hurried breaks between three video calls and ten telephone conversations. Those who are serious about working on themselves must designate time to do so, just as many religions prescribe fixed "time-outs" in the form of prayer hours and religious holidays. Note, too, that these time-outs do not in fact cause the world to fall apart: afterward, things keep working just as they did before. To be less religious about it, as the motivational speaker Tony Robbins once said: "If you don't have ten minutes to yourself, you don't have a life."

Perhaps you've heard the old proverb "A journey of a thousand miles begins with a single step." You can apply such an approach to your practice of personal time out. Two scheduled hours per week is a good start—ideally in the same regular time slot, since this will make it easier to follow through on the intention. "Closed from 4 p.m. on Fridays," the sign on your virtual office door might read. If this time is invested properly, you'll find your personal freedom growing by orders of magnitude—just like a return on a sound business plan.

Become an Investor of Time in Your Own Cause

Anyone who invests money is interested in the return. Similarly, anyone who invests time and energy should be keen to understand what they will get back. There will never be more than twenty-four hours in a day; thus, time is a limited and precious commodity. When I ask clients where they invest their money, almost all of them can answer me immediately and very specifically; in fact, I often get some handy investment tips. When I ask them where they invest their time, though, many struggle to reply. "I can't give a cut-and-dried answer to that," they say of their personal time investment portfolio. Here, therefore, is my own investment tip.

Take stock! Devote the first two hours of your new "free time" to carrying out a calendar analysis and understanding better where your time and energy are being spent.

Exercise: A Calendar Analysis

- Note down how you spend your time over a period of five weeks. Enter the times spent on each activity in the following table. Estimates are sufficient.
- Calculate how much time, on average, you spend on each activity per week and per day over the five weeks.

A calendar analysis

ACTIVITY		Number of hours in an average week					Average per week over five weeks	Average per day
		Week 1	Week 2	Week 3	Week 4	Week 5		
Working time	External meetings							
	Internal meetings							
	One-on-one conversations							
	Time for oneself							
	Breaks							
	Other							
Leisure time	Family							
	Exercise							
	Other							
Travel time								
Vacation								
Sleep								
TOTAL								

Now compare your results. Harvard Business School professor Michael E. Porter and former dean Nitin Nohria analyzed the calendars of a number of successful CEOs (Porter and Nohria 2018). Participants in the study averaged about six hours of personal time and just under seven hours of sleep per day. Of the personal time, about half was spent with family, forty-five minutes on exercise, and just over two hours on reading and hobbies. Of the work time, 25 percent was taken as alone time for activities such as reflection and preparing for meetings. The reflection time was described as particularly important for the study subjects' personal development.

- Consider the following questions: How much personal downtime do you have for leisure? How much for sleep? How much for yourself? How much do you want to have for each of these areas in the future?

My investment tip
Working time has diminishing marginal returns. In practical terms, this means that with every hour of additional work, you produce less output compared to the previous hour. Measured in terms of output, a three-hour night shift is as productive as one hour of morning work after adequate sleep. This is due to decreased nocturnal energy levels. With this in mind, it makes sense to manage your energy in the first instance, rather than your time. You can do so by giving structure and rhythm to your workday.

Giving Your Day Structure and Rhythm

"Have you ever thought how amazing it is that our hearts beat for our entire lives? The secret is in the rhythm, the synergy of activity and breaks," a cardiologist once explained to me. By following this principle and aligning our work routine with our body's natural rhythm, we can manage our own energy better. Science suggests that we should aim to work in ninety-minute cycles with breaks in between. As a client of mine once put it: "Each unit of work should be equivalent to a football match without extra time."

Sleep research shows that the basic rest-activity cycle runs in a ninety-minute rhythm divided into states of excitement and rest (Kleitman 1982).

This cycle occurs during both sleep and wakefulness. During periods of excitement, our concentration is significantly higher. Since the brain requires more energy than any other organ in the body, it "shuts down" if we concentrate hard enough for long enough. We then feel tired or unfocused. If we continue to push through these feelings, we trigger a stress response and the body switches to survival mode. It's not for nothing, then, that we're advised to take breaks between work sessions and enjoy a short walk or other relaxing activity. As a meditation teacher once told me: "If you think you can't spare thirty minutes for a break, you probably need sixty minutes of rest."

Our energy levels can be optimized still further, I learned from a top manager. He had welcomed me to the office in his sports gear. "Like a priceless work of art, a successful day should be framed properly—with morning and evening routines," he said. He told me how he rode his road bike to work three times a week: "I feel better when I recharge my batteries before tackling the prices on the stock exchange." He explained how he ended the day with an evening routine or an hour of "me-time" to wind down and prepare for sleep. He usually used this time to read, he said—and never for opening the laptop. As Arianna Huffington succinctly puts it: "A good morning begins the night before" (Matthes and Rickens 2021)—and after a good night's sleep, of course.

One Fine Wednesday at the Office

"Isn't this nice!" a colleague exclaimed, as we met at the office printer late one Wednesday evening. "Only four more hours of sleep, and it'll be the weekend again!" I always smile when I think back to that anecdote, though the topic itself is no laughing matter. In twenty years as a management consultant, I learned to get by on very little sleep. At times, I slept less than five hours a night on average.

I now know that this was entirely misguided. Philosopher Arthur Schopenhauer is credited with saying, "Sleep is to man what winding up is to a clock." Sleep is vital for our regeneration, and we need six to nine hours of it in order to be in the healthy range (Cappuccio et al. 2010). Few of us would argue that sleep is worth investing in: it's probably one of the most important energy sources of all. So far, so familiar. But how do we manage to build sufficient time for downtime into an already overcrowded workday?

"ATMs": Learning from the Masters of Time Management

Time management is an evergreen theme in business literature. Virtually all of us are familiar with the classic time management tools of define, prioritize, eliminate, simplify, delegate, and automate. Over the years, I've met a number of managers—masters of time management—who have honed these tools to perfection. I like to refer to these as "ATMs": advanced time managers. They take regular time for themselves with all the apparent ease of taking cash from an ATM. They can be found in DAX/Dow Jones corporations and in start-ups, boardrooms, and middle management. There is always something to be learned by observing ATMs in practice.

Define

Creating room means focusing only on what really matters. ATMs are clear about their goals. They use these goals to derive purposeful actions and don't allow themselves to be diverted from their course. The best ATMs can express a goal in a single word and place a laser focus on achieving it.

Prioritize

When it comes to time management theory, almost everyone knows the difference between important and urgent. ATMs devote 65 to 80 percent of their time to tasks that are important but not urgent, much like Stephen Covey, the thought leader in personal effectiveness, recommends (Covey 1994). When I explained this principle using the following diagram, some of my clients thought I had mislabeled the axes. They were mistaken.

Radical rethinking is required in order to prioritize successfully. I have met ATMs who took up to two months off for their families during the intense start-up phase of a new business. In every case, the business was a success.

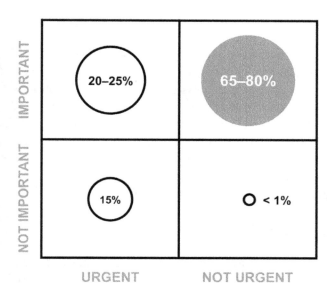

Prioritizing correctly (Source: Covey 1994)

Eliminate

Many managers report being frustrated by an overload of meetings and a daily influx of media and press reports. ATMs do what is necessary to avoid this. They deactivate disruptions, systematically eliminate "time sinks," and routinely say no. One ATM I met had introduced fixed office hours, outside of which he was not available. "By saying no, I'm saying yes to myself," he explained.

Simplify

"Simplicity is the ultimate sophistication," Leonardo da Vinci is thought to have said. ATMs avoid "unnecessary perfectionism" and work consistently according to the Pareto principle, which states that 80 percent of the output from a given situation is achieved with 20 percent of the total input. One ATM I knew made a habit of sitting down at the end of each week and asking which outputs could have been achieved with less effort. In this way, he gradually reduced his necessary working time until he had one full day off per week.

Delegate and Automate

ATMs are true masters of delegation and automation. They achieve this using modern optimization tools such as Asana.com or Monday.com as well as by taking advantage of the many digital services—from virtual assistance to market analysis—offered via online marketplaces such as Fiverr.com (https:// www.fiverr.com/). Asana's software helps teams and groups organize, track, and manage their work or projects (https://asana.com/de), while Monday .com is designed for managing projects and visualizing goals (https://www .monday.com/). In addition, many ATMs implement the advice given in the best-selling book *The 4-Hour Workweek* (Ferriss 2015).

A Fascinating Discovery

I have observed that, in practice, many managers find it difficult to create and protect time for themselves. Many don't immediately succeed in copying the ATM best practices just described. What's going wrong? When I looked at this with my engineer hat on, I made a fascinating discovery.

Picture your calendar as a tall wall built of solid stone blocks, each representing an appointment. If we pull out a block, the gap is immediately closed again by the downward force of the several-ton blocks above it. To create a stable opening, we need to construct an arch. We can imagine time management tools as the stones that form the arch. The final crucial piece—and in my experience, the one that's often missing—is the keystone. Only once this is present does the whole structure become sustainable long-term. In this analogy, the keystone is a well-thought-out incentive system that dissuades us from filling up our planned downtime with work meetings again.

Almost all the ATMs I've met over the years use an incentive system as a keystone and, by doing so, avoid a majestic archway being reduced to rubble again just a few weeks later. Some find it helpful to visualize their results by noting down whether they kept the space free each week. Smartphone apps are one way to do this. Other ATMs follow a similar approach to Sarah's, asking a friend to check in on the status of their intention. Some arrange to spend their time off in a place that inspires them; others fill the time with personal commitments that are impossible to cancel. Virtually all of them remind themselves regularly why they wanted to move down a gear in the first place. If we want to succeed in protecting our personal time, we must create a keystone to encourage us.

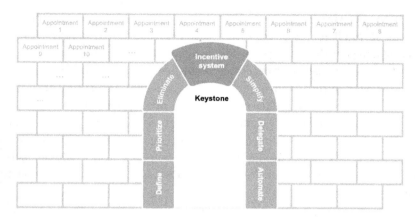

Creating and maintaining space in the calendar

Attentiveness: Taking Back Control of Our Thoughts

Let's imagine that you've finally managed to schedule some personal down-time. You've blocked off your diary and turned off your cell phone. You can't be reached. Suddenly, however, you remember that you wanted to call a customer back, you forgot to send out some documents, and you're a bit concerned about the upcoming restructuring. It seems this time-out isn't going to work—at least as far as mentally disengaging goes. You heeded the warning light, drove into the breakdown lane—and now the engine won't stop. What now?

A Hostile Takeover: When Thoughts Run Riot

"Stop worrying so much!" You've probably heard this advice more than once when confiding in a trusted friend about your problems. As you'll also know, it's not so easy to put into practice. We are taught to walk, talk, and read, but no one teaches us how to control our thoughts. What's worse, thought control frequently feels like a hopeless endeavor. Our head not only resists our orders, it often does the exact opposite of what we want it to do. American psychologist and Harvard professor Daniel Wegner proved this with his famous "white bear" experiment (Wegner et al. 1987), in which participants were instructed *not* to think of a white bear. If you attempt it yourself, you'll almost certainly fail. As a Zen master once told me, "If you try to stop your thoughts, you'll only make them more persistent."

The situation becomes especially problematic when our thoughts move outside our control and involuntary negative thought patterns recur incessantly, driven by chains of baseless assumptions. "If this and this happens, I may as well write off my career," "I'll never make it," and "I know what they think of me" are sentiments I hear time and again from my coachees. Generalizations are made, negative conclusions are drawn without evidence, sweeping assertions are formed on the basis of one data point, and the worst is always assumed.

The bad news is that negative thoughts can't simply be blocked or ignored: plain biology makes sure of this. It is possible, however, to learn how to deal with negative thoughts differently and to bring them back under our control. To do this, we need the ability to observe our thoughts with a mixture of courage and curiosity and a willingness to rest in our vital center.

Psychotherapist Karlfried Graf Dürckheim spoke in this regard of *hara*, our inner center of gravity, which grounds, strengthens, and rejuvenates us (Dürckheim 2012). The hara can be visualized as the center of a seesaw, the fixed balancing point that remains still amidst the constant up-and-down of the outer edges. This visual concept of the hara can be readily transferred to the world of thoughts and feelings, whereby the edges of the seesaw represent the emotional ups and downs that can be triggered by external successes and failures. Individuals who rest in their vital center—their hara—aren't buffeted up and down but can observe external goings-on from a safe distance. How can we learn to do this?

Mindfulness, Meditation, and More

A few years ago, a well-known industrial group invited me to give a talk along with two co-speakers. We were to speak at the annual senior managers' conference on the topic of mindfulness in business. The talk included a short meditation exercise in which we asked participants to focus solely on their breath for ninety seconds. Afterward, we asked who had managed it. Not a single hand was raised. When we then asked who would like to learn to do so, almost all sixty participants expressed interest.

Breathing and concentration techniques are experiencing burgeoning popularity, including within the walls of corporate boardrooms. They are particularly favored in the tech industry; Google, for example, launched its own "Search Inside Yourself" program a few years ago (Tan 2012). Mindfulness is also much talked about, although the term, in my view, is already somewhat played out. Concentrating on breath is a simple way to help train our attention and focus—a skill that we can later apply to managing our thoughts in order to build stress resilience. Studies show that these techniques can even improve leadership skills such as clarity and empathy (Schootstra, Deichmann, and Dolgova 2017).

There are now a number of apps offering self-guided meditations, including Insight Timer, Calm, Headspace, and 7Mind. To get you started, here's an exercise you can try right now.

Exercise: A Short Meditation

- Find a comfortable sitting position in which your body can relax. On a chair is best. Your back and head should be straight, your shoulders relaxed, and your hands clasped under your navel. Close your eyes if you wish.
- Focus your attention only on your breath. Feel it flow in and out through your nose. Let your breath happen.
- Notice when your mind wanders and bring it gently back to your breath. Simply watch what happens; don't judge.
- Now let yourself relax as you exhale, feeling the abdominal area below your navel. Keep focusing on your breath.
- Come back to the room slowly and open your eyes.

The more often you do this exercise, the better you'll get at focusing on your breath. Start with ninety seconds and add thirty seconds each day until you are meditating for ten minutes at a time. Incorporate the exercise into your morning routine and lunch break. Ten minutes twice a day is a good first goal to aim for.

On Becoming a Thought Tamer

The meditation technique just described can be used in a slightly modified form to bring racing thoughts back under control. The key here is that instead of observing our breath, we must observe our thoughts and feelings. Psychologist Susan David refers to this skill as "emotional agility" and proposes a technique whereby as soon as the first negative thought patterns appear, we should explicitly identify them as thoughts alone (David 2016). In this approach, "I may as well write off the business year" becomes simply "I've just had the thought that I may as well write off the business year." This is quite effective because it clearly shows our thoughts for what they are: temporary data sets in the head that flow by like water in a river. Seen from the meta level, many negative thoughts immediately lose their power.

In the next step, we must accept our thoughts and their associated feelings. Saying, "Things are what they are, and that's okay" could be a way to vocalize this intention. Such a statement creates distance between the thoughts and ourselves. With a little distance, new ways of seeing things emerge: a supposed failure might become a wake-up call. This is how a client of mine realized it was time for a change—and was ultimately grateful for what had forced him to confront it.

Of course, there will also be situations in which this approach is not effective. It takes time to learn to control one's thoughts: I know this from many conversations with clients. Moreover, in the right dose, it's healthy for our thoughts to occasionally give us pause. "A little paranoia is part of the basic emotional equipment of every manager," a board member once remarked to me. "It keeps you alert and quick to react."

In a nutshell:

- Learn to be attentive to your feelings in your daily work. They will send the first signals when something isn't right.
- Take physical signals like fatigue seriously and take steps to shift down a gear.
- Learn to listen to your gut and be aware of your body. This will help you make better decisions.
- Schedule at least two hours of personal downtime every week. Be unavailable to others during this time. Use it for reflection.
- Manage your energy, not your time. Work in ninety-minute cycles and take breaks in between.
- Free up space in your calendar by managing your time efficiently. Protect free space by finding your personal "keystone."
- Meditate for ten minutes twice a day. Mindfulness and meditation will help strengthen your vital center.
- Learn to notice, name, and accept your negative thoughts and feelings in order to regain control.

For the Curious among You: Where Sarah Is Now

Sarah has continued working on herself and is improving at managing her well-being all the time. These changes came at a key moment: she has since married and started a family. As a result, her priorities have shifted once again. She has progressed in her career at the company, taking over a new technical department and being proposed internally as a possible candidate for the executive board. Today, she is highly skilled at making space for her private life and managing her energy. While her world is certainly not perfect—for Sarah, combining career and family comes with all the usual challenges—she is considered a role model and serves as a mentor to young female engineers in her organization.

Resolve: Untangling Cause and Effect

When an engine light flashes, it is usually not possible to immediately determine the fault at hand. In many cases, it is the information from the diagnostic tool that provides the first real clues as to the components to be inspected during troubleshooting.

—AUTOMOBILE MAGAZINE AUTOBILD, 2021

Complex technical problems and personal quandaries have something in common—namely, in order to solve the problem, first you must understand the cause. In neither case can you settle for the "best available" answer. Indeed, this is where our second career stopper lurks—in blind spots and an unawareness of our own driving forces. It's not enough to know that the warning light is on; to find the cause, we must persistently follow all lines of inquiry. Surprising things may come to light during the process, as Michael's story shows.

Case Study: Michael

"I've been really looking forward to our coaching session," says Michael, pouring us a coffee. "It's the first time I've managed to escape the circus for more than an hour this week."

The Background

Michael and I are meeting today for our second coaching session. As a successful IT entrepreneur with his own security software company, Michael has carved out and fulfilled a niche. His company is the market leader in his segment in the German-speaking world. Unfortunately, sales have stagnated in the recent period and the company's lengthy spell of initial success appears to be drawing to an end. The company faces a major reorganization. It is against this background that Michael is seeking to rethink his role as CEO: going forward, he wants to delegate tasks and focus on the company's strategy. He has thus far failed to make these plans a reality, finding himself trapped deep in the mire of day-to-day business with no time to address strategic matters at all. Pressure is slowly cranking up. The goal of our coaching is to develop a plan to reset his priorities and structure his week differently and better.

Holding On at Any Cost

"It sounds as though your good intentions have fallen by the wayside again," I say to Michael. "You wanted to start taking two hours for strategy on a Friday. How's that going? Have you managed it?"

"Unfortunately not," he replies. "I'd planned to pull out of some internal meetings to create space in my schedule. There's no need for me to be there every time; my colleagues should know how to handle things by now. That's what I thought, anyway."

"And?" I ask.

"Well, then I found out that the meetings weren't going as planned. There were lots of unanswered questions about the construction of our new development center; it seemed like everyone was out of their depth. We'd also made no progress with the planning of the subsidiary in the Netherlands. So once again, I've taken care of things myself."

"And worked yet another eighty-hour week," I say.

"Yes, unfortunately. Meetings all day, evenings at my desk," says Michael, with a sigh. "I don't seem to be able to delegate anything. As always, my problem is that I only have twenty-four hours in a day and seven days in a week. There's just too much to do."

"Could it be," I ask, "that perhaps you don't want to delegate the work at all?"

"What do you mean?"

"In the 360-degree interviews, several people expressed doubt that you would ever really be able to step back. You would always have a tight grip on things; everybody in the company knew that, they said."

"I don't know who said that," he replies, "but it's an overstatement. I'm just trying to keep things from falling apart. If I don't step in, nothing gets done."

As part of our coaching, I had conducted 360-degree interviews with selected executives in the company and asked them about their view of Michael as a person. The goal was to help Michael better understand how he's perceived as a CEO and what blind spots he might have about his own behavior. These interviews had revealed significant differences between Michael's perceptions of himself and how he was perceived by others. The results of the interviews were consistent with a personality test we had conducted previously.

The Fear of Failure

"Do you remember the results of your personality test?" I ask. "They also suggested a pronounced desire for control."

"I just prefer to cast an eye over things before they leave the building."

"And what if you didn't do that? What then?"

"Everything would descend into chaos," comes the immediate reply.

"What do you mean by 'everything'?"

"The company," he says, "just everything I've built." As he says this, he suddenly looks very nervous.

"Isn't that a bit of an exaggeration?" I am surprised at the extremity of his response. "Why would the whole company immediately collapse just because you delegated a bit of responsibility? Aren't you taking more of a risk by doing everything yourself and leaving no time to worry about strategy?"

Michael falls silent for a moment and looks out the window. "You know," he begins, "sometimes I get into a real panic. I can't explain it. I get scared that I might fail and lose everything. It sounds crazy, but I lie awake at night thinking about how long I'd be able to support my family if money suddenly stopped coming in."

"But why would that be the case?" I ask. "You've built a successful company; you would always be able to build another one. The people around you admire your entrepreneurial talent."

"I think I've just been lucky," he says dismissively.

"But you would have had quite a lot of luck, if that were the case. Statistically speaking, it's rather unlikely. Aren't you proud of what you've achieved?"

Michael is silent for a moment, then speaks somewhat hesitantly. "Of course, there are moments where I'm proud. But there are also moments where I feel bad, and then I'm angry at myself *because* I feel bad."

"Can you say more about that?"

"It's a long story," he says. His face is sad. "My father was never proud of what I do. He wanted me to go to medical school and become a doctor like him and like my two siblings. He didn't think much of entrepreneurs, of moneymakers, as he used to say. I was always the black sheep of the family. Really, he was just waiting for me to fail as a business owner, like he used to wait for me to fail at school." His expression hardens and his voice turns angry. "But I've left all that in the past. For me, there's no more to be said on the subject."

"And now you've stepped into your father's shoes and you're waiting for yourself to fail?"

"What makes you say that?" he asks, surprised.

"Because you don't trust yourself, despite the fact that you have every reason to. As long as you believe that your success is down to luck, your trust in yourself is on shaky ground. And if you don't trust yourself, you can't trust others, and . . ."

". . . and then I end up being the ticket inspector of my own company," Michael interjects. "I'm compelled to go around checking up on everything all the time."

I laugh. "I wouldn't have expected you to poke fun at yourself like that."

"That doesn't come from me," he says dryly. "That comes from my wife. She tells me this every single day."

"Congratulations. You have a watchful observer by your side. Maybe you should listen to her more often."

"You're right. Apparently, there's some truth to what she's saying."

Unlearning a Compulsion for Control

Our coaching takes an interesting turn. In the weeks that follow, Michael becomes increasingly aware of how he contributes to his own time problem through a compulsion for control. We devise an action plan. Little by little, Michael succeeds in delegating a variety of tasks, although he finds it very difficult at first. This delegation frees up his time to focus on strategic matters. Finally, he makes an important decision about the direction of the company, which boosts his self-confidence. We meet for our final coaching session a few weeks later.

"I live on my own now," he begins.

"Have you separated from your wife?" I ask, concerned.

"No," he says. "I mean that my inner ticket inspector no longer resides in my head. I even canceled our final meetings without him managing to worm his way back in. I feel great, and I'm proud of myself."

"So now you have more time for strategy. Your competitors had better watch their backs!" We laugh.

What We Can Learn from Michael

▶ *Problems with performance aren't always due to the most obvious cause.*
Michael wanted to carve out time to work on his strategy. He set priorities and tried to delegate tasks. Unfortunately, due to an unconscious belief that things would fall apart unless he retained a tight grip on them, this attempt at prioritization and delegation was doomed to fail. He molded his world in such a way that the troublesome belief—"I can't trust anyone"—was constantly proven correct. The work ended up back on his desk. He sabotaged himself. His beliefs functioned like a random, forgotten segment of "ghost code" in his own operating system. What on the surface seemed like a performance or time management problem was actually a matter of personality.

▶ *Working on oneself begins with understanding one's personality.*
Michael was aware that he was a control freak. Previously, however, he had viewed this trait in a positive light, believing that it protected his company. Only by facing up to objective scrutiny of his behavior was he able to recognize the reality: that he was paying a high price for his beliefs in the form of working long hours and, far from protecting his company, he was jeopardizing it due to his urgent need for a well-considered strategy. This sudden realization played a pivotal role in Michael's commitment to intensive personal development. In this regard, Michael benefited from his pragmatic nature. Having recognized the problem, he wanted to address it directly.

▶ *It takes time to change one's behavior, just as it does to form it in the first place.*

It was the first time Michael had received such feedback, and it was difficult for him to accept it at first. I know from my own experience how painful this process can be. This feedback and the results of the personality test were the first clues in Michael's search for solutions. What makes Michael special is that he was determined to heed these clues and follow the trail. It's likely that Michael's inner ticket inspector has not in fact "moved out" completely, as Michael describes it, but rather that Michael is now better equipped to deal with it. Protective mechanisms such as striving for control are formed for a reason, especially if they arise from traumatic experiences. If an individual's degree of conviction in a belief is changed by only 2 percent, this in itself can be considered a success.

Keep reading to the end of the chapter to find out what happened to Michael next.

On Performance, Personality, and the Process of Becoming Ourselves

Every career has its turning points: times at which it seems like nothing is going right. Business is going poorly; performance reviews are unfavorable; we struggle to make sense of bad feedback. At these junctures, we have to dig deeper and "look under the hood." Understanding our personality helps us to ensure that we're addressing the true causes of problems, not just the symptoms. What might at first appear to be a time management or organization problem may in fact be related to the deep-seated beliefs we formed a long time ago. The following three questions can help us to work through this process:

- What do others recognize about my performance that I don't?
- In which areas do I act in accordance with my natural preferences, talents, and values? In which do I not?
- Which unconscious processes tend to steer me in the wrong direction? How can I get back on course?

The next section is all about answering these questions.

Performance: How Our Effort Is Measured

Almost all modern companies use their own competency models to develop and evaluate employees. I used my firm's competency model to advise consultants on their career development for more than ten years. Professional services firms, in particular, put a great deal of effort into employee development. This is part of the business model, because employees are the currency of competition in the sector. Whichever firm "wins" and develops the most talent will also win in a business sense. All HR development programs are founded on regular objective feedback that helps employees to recognize their own strengths and weaknesses and to improve accordingly. However, this requires that the feedback is accepted and understood and that the employees concerned are able to implement it. How does this play out in practice?

Identity vs. Reputation

There are two stories told about our performance and success. One is the story we tell ourselves; the other is the one that is told about us. It is against this background that Robert Hogan, an American psychologist known for his innovations in the field of personality assessments, defines personality from two perspectives: identity and reputation (Hogan and Kaiser 2005).

Identity is what he calls the "actor's view": how we see ourselves. For example, someone who is convinced they have played a significant role in a business deal might judge themselves to be successful. "I make everything happen," they say confidently. From an observer's point of view, however, the story might look different. Perhaps that person's colleagues view the circumstances that led to the business deal quite differently; maybe the individual's conspicuous display of confidence isn't substantiated by reality and serves only to confirm his reputation for taking himself a little too seriously. "Did you see him doing that again?" the colleagues say, behind closed doors.

Base Jumpers, Wrong-Way Drivers, and Eternal Sailors

Those who are receptive and open to feedback are able to reconcile their identity with their reputation and learn important lessons. Feedback typically takes the form of regular performance reviews, 360-degree interviews, or informal feedback from other colleagues in management roles. Ideally, competencies and skills should be assessed and these assessments backed up by concrete observations and suggestions for improving the subject's way of doing things.

Things get tricky when a persistent discrepancy forms between identity and reputation. I've come to recognize three types of personalities to whom this typically happens.

Base Jumpers

You might have heard the story of the person who jumps off the roof and, caught in a nosedive, calls out to the people on the second floor that everything's going well so far. This is what happens when naive optimistic types do not receive feedback. They develop a blind spot (see https://en.wikipedia.org/wiki/Johari_window) and, in the absence of evidence to the contrary, convince themselves that all is going swimmingly. Then, when they fail to progress to the next rung of their career or their contract isn't renewed, reality comes like a blow. This category includes lateral hires who fail due to a lack of feedback on the cultural stumbling blocks in a new company. In its broadest manifestation, this group also includes highly talented neurotic types or insecure overachievers for whom precisely the reverse applies: they're objectively among the best, but a lack of external reassurance leads them to conclude that they don't meet the demands of the role and have obtained it merely through luck. This is why they often work until they drop—perhaps not only figuratively.

Wrong-Way Drivers

You've probably heard the joke about the wrong-way driver on the highway. When a friend calls to warn them that there's a wrong-way driver on the loose, the driver says, "I know! There's not just one—there are hundreds of them!" This is the feeling experienced by many who cannot or will not accept feedback. They perceive themselves to be unfairly judged and increasingly sidelined. However, this category also includes those who acknowledge the validity of the feedback they receive, but no longer feel inclined to assign it any real importance. They have ceased to identify with the organization's values and goals; in their head, they've already handed in their resignation letter. They no longer display the outward enthusiasm of days gone by, and might well be thinking about a job change.

Eternal Sailors

Imagine a newly promoted sea captain who continues to act like a sailor. Instead of ascending to the bridge and taking command, they continue to simply scrub the deck; after all, this is what they know they're good at. This is what happens to those who recognize the value of the feedback they receive but are unable to put it into practice. They fall back on familiar patterns of behavior and grasp at their supposed strengths—things that may have made them successful in the past, but are now becoming part of the problem. Such people run faster and faster in the wrong direction, struggling all the while, until at some point they simply can't go on. Changing things requires understanding the root cause of their behavior. If they can't do this, they're probably in the wrong job—as reluctant as they may be to admit it.

What If Feedback Isn't Possible?

Feedback is a gift that not everyone is lucky enough to receive. As part of a lecture at IESE Business School in Barcelona, I worked with MBA students to identify sources of objective feedback for entrepreneurs who typically don't have a chance to obtain it. A fantastic range of sources were proposed, from a personal "mastermind group"—a carefully selected assortment of friends and experts—to a regular cab driver, a yearslong acquaintance with whom the subject of the feedback talks about "everything." All of these options can help to reduce a blind spot. Ultimately, only those who receive feedback from a variety of sources at regular intervals can recognize where their reputation and identity diverge and work on themselves accordingly. Doing so is a reliable way to bring the two back into alignment.

I am well aware—from discussions with clients as well as from my own experience—that it becomes increasingly difficult to obtain objective feedback as you move up each rung of the career ladder. If at some point you find that the feedback you receive has become exclusively positive, alarm bells should start to ring. Factors such as fear or flattery may have created a distorted picture of your strengths and weaknesses in others' supposedly objective observations. This renders their feedback worthless. As it happens, this is often the price that must be paid for advancement in your chosen career path.

When was the last time you received feedback? If it's been a while, the following exercise may be of use to you.

Exercise: Actively Seeking Feedback

Take a moment to study the following criteria:

	1	2	3	4	5
Problem-solving and analytical skills	☐	☐	☐	☐	☐
Strategic thinking	☐	☐	☐	☐	☐
Results driven	☐	☐	☐	☐	☐
Action oriented	☐	☐	☐	☐	☐
Value generation and business development	☐	☐	☐	☐	☐
Expertise and idea generation	☐	☐	☐	☐	☐
Presence, gravitas, and influence	☐	☐	☐	☐	☐
Presentation skills, communication, and cooperation	☐	☐	☐	☐	☐
Leadership skills	☐	☐	☐	☐	☐
Teaming	☐	☐	☐	☐	☐
People development	☐	☐	☐	☐	☐
Political savvy	☐	☐	☐	☐	☐
Client and relationship management	☐	☐	☐	☐	☐
Project management	☐	☐	☐	☐	☐

Which criteria are relevant for your role? Once you have selected the relevant items, use them as a basis for self-evaluation. How often do you demonstrate your abilities in these areas?

5 = Always
4 = Often
3 = Frequently
2 = Sometimes
1 = Rarely

Now pick two or three colleagues whom you trust and who know you well. Ask them to evaluate you based on these criteria. Where do their evaluations diverge from your own? What can you learn from this?

Personality: What Makes Us . . . Us

As a young consultant, I was regularly told that I was too quiet in client meetings and needed to be more visible. Acting on this feedback didn't come particularly easily to me, as I tend to be a quiet and calm person by nature. A colleague of mine, on the other hand, was perceived as too dominant. At the beginning, he, too, found it difficult to know what to do with this information: it wasn't in his nature to hold back. There's a part of each of us that appears to be inborn and independent from our acquired knowledge and skills, but is nevertheless of pivotal significance when it comes to carving out a career. Humans have been attempting to wrangle with this part for over two thousand years.

What Remains of the Alps When the Mountains Are Gone

As early as 360 BC, Hippocrates distinguished between four "temperaments": sanguine, melancholic, choleric, and phlegmatic. We encounter these four types again and again in literature and film, from Shakespeare to *Star Wars*. The word *temperament* refers to our innate and unchangeable inclinations and preferences. In a figurative sense, it is "what remains of the Alps when the mountains are gone," as a fellow coach once told me.

There's a distinction to be drawn between character and temperament. Our character is formed over the course of our lives and includes, in addition to our temperament, the habits we have been taught or that we have taught ourselves. Personality, which is different again, can be thought of as the sum total of the traits, inclinations, behaviors, and beliefs that make us who we are. An individual with a well-formed personality might be defined as one with distinctive, clearly identifiable traits and characteristics; one who has insight into their strengths, weaknesses, and talents and is willing to defend them, even if those around them tend to perceive them as negative. When describing and evaluating someone's personality, many of us also factor in aspects of a person's physical appearance.

Finally, Data on the Table!

My own personal development journey involved a number of interesting discoveries. Among the most fascinating to me was the fact that the unchangeable part of one's personality—one's inborn temperament—could be measured in a standardized way. Having signed up to attend a training course for project leaders, I, along with the other attendees, was required to take a personality test beforehand. Our individual results were confidentially shared with each of us during the session. *Finally, data on the table!* I thought. My engineer's heart beat faster. Alas, the four-letter result didn't take the form of numbers, as I had hoped, yet it nevertheless represented something tangible. It was something I could finally get my teeth into. We had taken what is known as the Myers-Briggs Type Indicator (MBTI) test (see https://eu.themyersbriggs.com/), in which participants decide between two preferences within each of four dichotomies:

- Where do you get your energy (extraversion vs. introversion)?
- How do you take in information (sensing vs. intuition)?
- How do you make decisions (thinking vs. feeling)?
- How do you interact with the outside world (judging vs. perceiving)?

The answers to these questions give rise to sixteen possible combinations representing the sixteen personality types (Lorenz and Oppitz 2015).

Upon taking my first MBTI test, I felt as though someone had given me the instruction book for myself. Not only did I learn that parts of my personality are not changeable at all—or if they are, only with great difficulty—but I also learned about how these unchangeable preferences influence the things that come easily to me and those I find more challenging. That was an insight I could immediately apply.

As a consultant, for example, I was required to learn to sell. I had long hated this part of the job. *I'm just not a natural salesperson*, I used to tell myself. I attended the usual training courses, but to no avail: when I was encouraged to "get out of my shell," I frequently felt that I was literally standing outside of myself. The MBTI test led me to an important revelation, namely that my previous efforts had been focused in the wrong direction entirely. I am an introvert. I had been aware of this before, but now I had it in writing. I began to focus my attention on exploiting my "introvert strengths": listening, observing closely, projecting a sense of calm. Suddenly things were different—and better: I prioritized engaging clients in personal, meaningful conversations. I no longer battled with the self-imposed pressure of having to sell something at any cost. Projects materialized as if of their own volition; I discovered new sources of energy to tap on a daily basis.

Many of the clients who come to me have taken an MBTI test in the past, but not all of them remember the result. Even fewer consciously consider this result in their efforts to initiate behavioral change. This is a pity, because revisiting one's result at periodic intervals can be a valuable asset for personal development. I've found the test to be equally worthwhile in the context of developing a leadership team. In one instance, when I was tasked with improving team performance in a professional services team, I facilitated a workshop where each attendee presented their personal MBTI profile and, in doing so, revealed their personal "instruction book" to their colleagues. This required a great deal of courage and openness from all participants. As a result, however, it helped to build trust in the team and to reinvent the way team members engaged with one another.

Learning to See: How Do We Close a Blind Spot?

"The two biggest barriers to good decision-making are your ego and your blind spots," wrote entrepreneur and hedge fund manager Ray Dalio (2019). As verified by countless conversations with coaching clients, personality tests work very well in conjunction with feedback as a means of closing these blind spots. They provide a largely objective view of the test-taker and can help them make better sense of their past successes and failures. There is often an "aha!" moment when patterns and relationships between personality and behavior suddenly start to emerge.

Personality tests can be a great starting point to convince even skeptics of the value of working on oneself. They may suspect that there's a problem but find it difficult to grapple with their moods and feelings. "I don't have time for this emotional stuff," a client once said to me. Since skeptics often prefer to deal with hard numbers, data, and facts, a standardized personality test's claim to scientific legitimacy may be the thing that succeeds in overcoming their resistance. I know what I'm talking about. As an avowed mechanical engineer, I was part of this club for a long time myself.

Welcome to the Labyrinthine World of Personality Testing

"Are you INTJ, too?"

"No idea. I'm blue. Is INTJ blue?"

"Don't know. Has it got something to do with the blue Hogan test?"

"The MVPI? No, that's something else. I've only done the yellow Hogan test."

"Oh yes, the HPI. That's a bit like the Big Five. Have you done the red test, as well?"

"The HDS? Not yet, unfortunately. . . ."

This is an imagined conversation between two high-potential hires following the completion of various personality tests as part of a young talent development program. The dialogue illustrates that in the world of personality tests—a key tool in the field of psychometrics—it's easy to lose sight of the big picture. Hundreds of tests and assessments exist under this umbrella, ranging from simple tests in magazines—which often have only limited significance—to scientific instruments that are generally accurate at predicting human behavior. For a personality test to produce a meaningful result, clear criteria apply. It must be objective; it must capture information about elements of personality that are stable over time, not transient mood states; it must produce repeatable results; and it must actually measure what it claims to measure.

Determining which test makes sense in a particular instance depends entirely on the individual need. Does the test-taker have a decision to make about the direction of their career or how to best develop their strengths? Are they seeking to discover their blind spots as a CEO or work better in a team? I have used a variety of personality tests in my work over the years. Some of the scientific personality tests are available and easily accessible to anyone, in some cases free of charge. What follows are a few recommendations based on my personal experience, but this list is by no means exhaustive.

Myers-Briggs Type Indicator Test: The Beginner's Model

Described in some detail in the previous pages, the MBTI test is frequently used in the development of managerial talent. Though it isn't fully consistent with more recent psychological findings and thus some aspects of its approach are now considered controversial, its accessible four-letter result has an enduring appeal. For this reason, the test is still widely used in the business world. The internet is jam-packed with forum discussions about Steve Jobs's purported MBTI profile and which profile a person should have to become a successful entrepreneur. The extended version (step II) of the MBTI test delves deeper into the twenty facets of personality. To take the MBTI test, you'll need an appropriately certified coach or trainer through whom you can access the test and who will help you understand the results.

Values in Action (VIA) Test: For Those Who Seek Authentic Happiness

In my experience, the VIA test is particularly valuable for personal career planning or decisions about one's professional direction. It is based on the research findings of US psychologists Martin Seligman and Chris Peterson, who have become known for their work in the field of "positive psychology." The test aims to determine the taker's character strengths and is based on the research-backed idea that knowledge and application of these strengths in daily life can help us achieve authentic happiness (Seligman 2005). Based on the test-taker's answers, the test ranks twenty-four character strengths by the degree to which they are exhibited; the top five are then taken as the test-taker's personal result. More than 750,000 people have taken the VIA test to date. It is available free of charge online.

Exercise: Getting to Know Your Character Strengths

Go to https://www.authentichappiness.sas.upenn.edu/testcenter, which offers free access to a number of tests. Fill out the free online VIA survey of character strengths. This will take about twenty-five minutes. The test will rank your character strengths and display your top five. You may be surprised by the results. The test is also available via the following link: https://www.viacharacter.org/.

StrengthsFinder Test: The Career Booster

This test can be useful when organizational change is on the agenda and the test-taker is seeking to uncover heretofore unused personal skills. Corporate reorganization is one such scenario. The test is based on studies by Gallup and, in my experience, is suitable for all management levels, including board level. It determines the test-taker's unique rank order for thirty-four themes, each of which is assigned to one of the four broader categories of executing, influencing, relationship building, and strategic thinking. The top five themes represent the test-taker's most strongly expressed natural talents. The best-selling book *Now, Discover Your Strengths* (Buckingham and Clifton 2016) provides a personal access code for the online test. A certified coach can also provide access to the more comprehensive Clifton-Strengths test, which reveals the ranking of all thirty-four themes rather than just the top five.

Keirsey Temperament Sorter: A Crash Course in Mind Reading

This test can be particularly helpful when it comes to decision-making regarding the appointment of candidates to leadership roles. Closely associated with the MBTI test, the Keirsey Temperament Sorter distinguishes between four basic temperaments, each of which is subdivided into four subtemperaments. The resulting sixteen variants correspond to the profiles in the MBTI test. The Temperament Sorter adopts catchy labels—Idealists, Rationals, Guardians, and Artisans—for the four basic temperaments. A test-taker's basic temperament can provide the first clue about the type of leadership role best suited for them, whether one centered on diplomacy (Idealists), strategy (Rationals), tactics (Artisans), or logistics (Guardians). If you've taken an MBTI test in the past, it's easy to transfer the results to Keirsey's model and determine your base temperament according to this system. A questionnaire can also be found in the book *Please Understand Me II* (Keirsey 1998).

Since Keirsey's model is based on observable personality traits, such as the use of abstract versus concrete language, you can also use it to interpret everyday work situations simply by watching and listening; a list of questions isn't explicitly required at all. A Rationalist, for example, might speak abstractly about the "impact of the COVID crisis on hygiene supply chains," whereas a Guardian would state explicitly, "We don't have toilet paper today." In conversations, these varying perspectives can provide initial clues about your counterpart's character. A coaching colleague from London brought the Keirsey Temperament Sorter to my attention a few years ago. Prior to that, I had always had the feeling that she could read minds. Today I know that her insights are the result of careful observations interpreted through the Keirsey model.

Herrmann Brain Dominance Instrument: Analyzing Thinking Styles

Based on the Whole Brain Thinking Model, the Herrmann Brain Dominance Instrument (HBDI) test is a modern variant of the four-category model just described. The HBDI test analyzes modes of thinking and distinguishes between the rational self, the organizing self, the feeling self, and the experimental self (https://www.thinkherrmann.com/hbdi). The four-type classification system exhibits some parallels with the Keirsey Temperament Sorter model. The instrument uses a simple color code to visualize results, with blue representing the rational self, green the organizing self, red the feeling self, and yellow the experimental self. The test can be taken only through certified providers.

DISC Personality Test: Predicting Behavior

While the DISC (dominant, influential, steady, and conscientious) personality test is also predicated on four basic categories, it's structured somewhat differently from the tests we've already discussed. Widely used in management, DISC assessments help test-takers to better understand their own behavior as well as that of the people they interact with. Similar to other tests, the DISC system uses a color code to visualize results: red for dominant, yellow for influential, green for steady, and blue for conscientious. In my experience, the DISC test is particularly helpful for working with leadership teams—where there's a need to better understand group dynamics, for example. This test is available free of charge online (see https://www.mydiscprofile.com/en-us/free-personality-test.php).

Hogan Leadership Forecast: The Rolls-Royce of Personality Tests

Based on the work of noted psychologist Robert Hogan, this test is particularly helpful for addressing questions about an individual's leadership style. It consists of three parts. The Hogan Personality Inventory (HPI) analyzes seven dimensions related to leadership performance using an approach based on the Big Five model from the field of personality psychology (see https://en.wikipedia.org/wiki/Big_Five_personality_traits). The Hogan Development Survey (HDS), or Challenge report, provides insights about personality-based performance risks and potential derailers such as the test-taker's reactions under high stress, whereby the findings are interpreted with reference to the neurobiological "fight-flight-freeze" response. Finally, the Motives, Values, Preferences Inventory (MVPI) explores the test-taker's goals, values, and preferences, providing insights into their personal drivers, leadership style, and more. In my experience, combining the comprehensive reports from all three assessments often yields surprising new information for leaders.

I recommend that you take at least two of these tests as part of your own initial "look under the hood." The results will likely enable you to connect pieces of the puzzle in ways that previously weren't apparent to you. You may even discover some clues to your most deeply held driving forces— those you've been unable to recognize and use thus far.

The Process of Becoming Ourselves: Why We Do What We Do

In a perfect world, our performance would precisely mirror our potential. At play, at work, and everywhere in between, we would be on the ball and achieving at our best. In the real world, we face interference that prevents us from doing so—and when this happens, it can feel like we're driving with one foot on the gas and the other on the brake. US sports coaching expert Timothy Gallwey described this phenomenon in his classic work *The Inner Game of Tennis* (Gallwey 1986), later expressing it in the following formula:

$$\text{Performance (P)} = \text{Potential (p)} - \text{Interference (i)}$$

Interference can sometimes manifest as the absence of necessary knowledge or skills. Often, however, it's due to an individual's mindset or inner attitude—feelings of insecurity or a lack of drive, self-confidence, or motivation. Such attitudes develop throughout an individual's life, beginning with their childhood experiences. Later, at turning points in their professional life, this interference acts as "ghost code" in their operating system, hindering their performance when it counts the most. Having experienced this phenomenon myself, I'll illustrate it using my own case study. In the spirit of honesty, I'll preface this by saying that my attempts to look into my own "engine compartment" could go only so deep.

The Story of an Inner Driver: A Play in Five Acts

Perhaps one of my greatest career challenges was attaining the mental readiness to ascend to partner in a major consulting firm. I had never learned so much about myself as I did during this process. For the first time in my professional life, I understood my innate driver behavior—and I became acquainted with heretofore unknown parts of my personality in the process. I would gladly have gone without meeting some of them.

Act One: The Inner Driver Rears Its Head

As part of the preparatory training for my new partner role, I had taken an array of personality tests and learned a great deal about myself. My

StrengthsFinder profile showed a clear tendency to be an Achiever. Indeed, that was how I defined myself: working hard and readily pulling all-nighters when needed. It was an inner driver that was there when it mattered: when I worked on the board presentation until 4 a.m. to make sure no detail was forgotten. I never questioned where this driver had come from or who had invited it to the party. Yet while it wasn't consciously summoned, its appearance followed a distinct pattern. If I secretly feared botching the presentation and making a fool of myself, there the inner driver would suddenly be. I was exhibiting the classic profile of an insecure overachiever.

While I had a hard time owning up to this fear, I couldn't deny the pattern. As I prepared for meetings with experienced leaders, its voice became relentless: *Let's not embarrass ourselves.* I felt compelled to anticipate every question in advance and to plan intelligent answers. The feedback I received as a partner spoke of a need for greater self-confidence and gravitas; I was not yet a "trusted advisor," as they say in the consulting world. This feedback seemed to reflect the pattern. Apparently, my insecurity was palpable to others.

My "solution" was to suppress my fear and ramp up my preparation. From now on, there would be no question to which I did not know the answer. This extra preparation, I thought, would boost my self-confidence and solve the issue. You might not be surprised to learn that the opposite transpired.

The more I tried to build a shield with preparation, the more insecure I became. I hid behind reams of slides in client meetings, perpetually afraid of being caught out. I decided I had to get to the bottom of things—and when I did, I discovered a treacherous psychological mechanism.

Act Two: An Unknown Side of Myself Emerges

Who or what within me actually feared these mistakes? It was a question I had pondered for some time. While I knew my inner driver all too well, there was another side of my personality—one I only vaguely sensed—that had remained buried for some time. As soon as it spoke up, my inner driver was there to hurry it away again. When this happened, the hidden side rebelled silently with fear, and my inner driver responded by upping its relentless campaign against me: *Work harder, work longer!* The two entered a cycle of perpetual motion: fear, performance, more fear, more performance. My reactions were programmed by this connection. "Neurons that fire together, wire together," as they say in neurobiology.

Suddenly I saw it clearly: it was the fear of making mistakes and failing that had driven me to succeed so far. This fear had spurred me to perform at the highest level and launched me to the top ranks of the firm with the thrust of a Saturn V rocket. A life-changing realization! At the same time, I thought, I had reached the end of where this driver could take me. For one thing, this brutal psychological mechanism would sooner or later have led to burnout; for another, it was incompatible with my role as partner. How could I face clients with confidence when I was driven by the fear of embarrassing myself? The two things were wholly contradictory. Unfortunately, there was no quick fix. For the time being, I had to content myself with continuing to explore my inner self and observing and understanding the connections better.

Act Three: A Plan Is Forged

Because my focus was on avoiding mistakes, it naturally followed that my self-confidence was completely contingent on external indicators of performance and success. If the content of a presentation was criticized, I perceived this as criticism of myself. If I was praised, my self-confidence rose. I craved recognition. *If you want to be perceived as a "go-to" partner in the market, you've got to sell big projects first,* I told myself. That was my belief. Later, a helpful conversation with an experienced colleague revealed that in fact, I had confused cause and effect. In order to be successful in business, I first had to be accepted by clients as an advisor who could meet them on equal ground, one with a knack for engaging and understanding them. To do that, I had to cultivate a sense of self-confidence that was completely divorced from my performance metrics.

This type of self-confidence arises from a sense that one belongs and yet is totally unique. It develops only when one takes a long look in the mirror and embraces oneself with all one's weaknesses. In this new mindset, I was no longer allowed to define myself by the opinions of others: I had to learn to speak my mind, regardless of whether or not a client agreed with me. But openly disagreeing with an important client, let alone the board? The very thought of it made me shudder. No sooner had I thought of it than my primal fear of failure reared its head again. There was only one solution: to face it head-on.

Act Four: The Inner Driver Makes a Fatal Mistake

As I set about trying to make these changes, my inner driver was more of a hindrance than a help. It was proving more and more to be an unwelcome presence, an uninvited guest with bad manners. It even seemed to have no qualms about attempting acts of sabotage: if I hadn't prepared a presentation to perfection, or if I planned—in a break from my previous form—to visit a client without my PowerPoint slides, it made me feel like I was on a kamikaze mission. It berated me internally, accusing me of jeopardizing everything it had ever accomplished for me. What was surprising was that the client meetings in question actually went very well. That should have emboldened me. The driver, however, didn't think much of celebrating success. It ignored the positives and looked for its next point of attack.

At this point, it had begun to rear its head during my leisure time, too. Whether I was playing golf or making music, I caught it setting lofty goals for me and relentlessly challenging me to do better. It took the fun out of things I had previously enjoyed. Yet by inserting itself so persistently, it had made a fatal error. Now I was wise to it.

As soon as I felt the enjoyment being sucked out of something, I knew the driver wouldn't be far away. I had identified the warning sign. Unbeknownst to the driver, I could now start to work on getting rid of it.

Little by little, I got in touch with a side of my personality that didn't care about performance at all. It was one I had long kept suppressed. This side wasn't so afraid of making mistakes; it seemed to take life a little more lightly. It was more open and creative, but also more vulnerable. When it was rebuffed, it reacted with fear. When it finally managed to get a word in edgewise, it had quite amazing ideas. *I have to take this side to my clients*, I thought to myself.

Act Five: The Enemy Becomes an Ally

And that's how it happened. Finally, I succeeded in letting this formerly hidden side speak up in a client meeting. I suddenly felt completely different. All at once, I found myself addressing a seasoned and respected leader with questions I would never have dared ask before. My previous fear of embarrassment was gone without a trace. Without preparation or Power-Point, we talked freely about strategy and organizational development; a planned forty-five-minute conversation turned into an almost three-hour one. The client asked me to quote a consulting project on such an ambitious scale that I was almost rendered speechless. My inner driver emerged again—but this time as a helper. Speaking in a friendly manner, it reassured me that a project of this magnitude was well within my capabilities. It inwardly patted me on the back and whispered, *Congratulations—well done.*

End Titles: My Inner Heroes, Then and Now

I have come to know more sides of my personality over the years, and they in turn have become good friends. They appreciate and complement one another. If one side becomes too dominant, another speaks up. Of course, like a band in a jam session, the sounds sometimes clash or don't work well together. Other days, they're in perfect rhythm and harmony. All these parts are me. Together, they are what makes up my personality.

Unconscious Processes and Self-Limiting Beliefs

Upon first reading, my play in five acts might well put the reader in mind of Robert Louis Stevenson's tale of Dr. Jekyll and Mr. Hyde. Yet in order to pursue personal growth as a leader, it's necessary—at certain points in your career—to take a closer look at the different sides of your personality. In this context, feedback and personality tests aren't sufficient: personality is too complex a matter for that. Neuroscience tells us that unconscious mental processes are of great significance in how we think and make decisions. It is because of these mental processes that we usually get what we unconsciously expect, even if we superficially claim that we want something completely different. This same phenomenon played out in Michael's case study. Here, self-limiting beliefs played an important role.

These types of beliefs usually stem from childhood experiences or from crises of meaning or purpose in our lives. They have to do with our basic psychological needs: for attachment and belonging, orientation and control, self-enhancement, and pleasure and avoidance of pain (Grawe 2012). We develop positive or negative beliefs depending on whether these basic needs have been fulfilled or violated in the past. In order to repress negative or traumatic experiences and avoid them being repeated, we develop protective mechanisms.

Michael's protective mechanism was a compulsion for control. In my case, a fear of mistakes had developed as a manifestation of my own protective mechanisms: perfectionism and the search for recognition. To become more credible and authentic as a leader, I had to find a way to leave them behind.

Unfortunately for us, changing our beliefs isn't as easy as deleting and replacing apps on a smartphone; they're an integral part of us. What's more, the protective mechanisms associated with these beliefs did, at one point, serve a worthwhile purpose. We developed them to protect ourselves. As a result, they behave like a **guardian** that blocks the door to our inner world. We can sometimes hear the voice of this guardian inside us. *You have to _____*, it says, or *If you don't do _____ right now, then _____ will happen!* Getting to know this guardian better requires us to observe ourselves.

Exercise: Recognizing and Challenging Self-Limiting Beliefs

To help you identify your self-limiting beliefs, ask yourself the following questions:

- What assumptions do you use to limit yourself? When do you say to yourself: *I have to _____, I should _____, I shouldn't _____, I can't _____, or I'd rather wait until _____*?
- What patterns can you recognize? Give them a name. What self-limiting beliefs do you think might be behind them?

Next, challenge your self-limiting beliefs. Author Nancy Kline proposes a very effective method for doing this (Kline 1999). Look at your negative beliefs again, then ask yourself the following questions:

- What if the opposites of these beliefs were true? What if *I have to* _____ became *I don't have to* _____ , and so on? What would you do? How would you feel?

Internalize this feeling and repeat this exercise at regular intervals. Over time, you will notice a positive change.

Dealing with Self-Limiting Beliefs

Timothy Gallwey developed a similarly effective technique for dealing with self-limiting beliefs in athletes. Though originally designed to be applied in a sports context, it lends itself very well to use in professional life. Within this technique, he conceives of the "outer" and "inner" games (Gallwey 1986). In the outer game, we work on our technique. In the inner game, we address our nervousness, self-doubt, and self-condemnation.

It is primarily victories won in the inner game, Gallwey says, that determine a person's success. He distinguishes between two sides of the self, whereby Self 1 can be thought of as the conscious "determiner," and Self 2 as the subconscious "doer." The two engage in an inner dialogue. Peak performance is achieved when Self 1 and Self 2 act in harmony, as I experienced in my successful client meeting. This harmony happens when we simply "let things happen" in a state of relaxed concentration without worrying about the results. The following steps are designed to achieve this:

1. Observing nonjudgmentally
2. Programming the self by imagining the desired outcome
3. Letting things happen without the conscious effort to exert control, while practicing nonjudgmental observation of the outcome

To understand how this might be applied in the workplace, let's imagine you want to appear more confident in important presentations. In this instance, your self-limiting belief might be that you can't present convincingly. In the first step, observe yourself during presentations without judging. In what specific ways do you act? How does this make you feel? Next, visualize how you want to come across. What posture, facial expressions, and gestures do you want to adopt? How fast do you want to talk? The more concrete the image you visualize, the better. Retrieve this desired image before your next presentation, then present without striving for conscious control and without judging. Your belief system will relinquish its grip and be temporarily deactivated—and the results will astonish you. The more successes you have, the more your self-limiting beliefs will lose their effect without you even thinking about it.

In a nutshell:

- The higher you climb on the career ladder, the less open and honest feedback you get. Always question yourself in a constructive yet critical manner.
- Take every opportunity you can to seek honest feedback and, in doing so, to bring your identity (self-perception) into harmony with your reputation (others' perception of you).
- Take a recognized personality test to learn more about your natural temperament and character.
- Seek to understand the extent to which you are currently acting or not acting in accordance with your preferences, talents, and values.
- Follow the clues revealed by your feedback and personality tests in order to pinpoint your self-limiting beliefs.
- Observe your "inner game" and challenge your self-limiting beliefs.

For the Curious among You: Where Michael Is Now

Michael's business is doing very well, due in no small part to his personal role in its development. He took time out to attend a two-week executive course at a leading business school following our coaching. Given his responsibilities as CEO, his willingness to do this was testament to his impressive personal growth. He is now much better able to let go than he used to be—notwithstanding the occasional "relapse," as he calls it, when he suddenly appears in the development department and starts firing off questions. To counter this, he blocks off fixed days that are devoted entirely to strategic work. His company benefits as a result.

Remove: Discarding Behaviors That No Longer Benefit Us

To add new oil, the old oil must first be removed. This is self-evident: it's why we refer to "changing the oil."

—Q&A PLATFORM GUTEFRAGE.NET

No combustion engine car can run without engine oil, since this is what cools and lubricates the engine. At some point, the oil becomes old and its useful properties are depleted. We can't simply pour the new oil on top, however; first, we must drain and dispose of the old oil in order to prevent damage to the engine. The same principle applies to our careers. Each career has turning points at which we must consciously discard previously successful tools, approaches, and patterns of behavior. The inability to do this represents our third career stopper. Those who can't let go are unable to move forward. Lucy's story illustrates just that.

Case Study: Lucy

It's Tuesday evening, and Lucy and I have an appointment for a video call. This is our third coaching session. Lucy and I have never met in person: the lockdowns are to thank for that. In the meantime, our virtual meetings have come to feel like second nature. As always, Lucy is perfectly on time. "I've been looking forward to our session," she says. "There's a lot to catch up on." Lucy sits comfortably at the table in her modern office; the ambience suits her character. On the wall behind her hangs an image reading "Women in Tech."

The Background

Lucy works for a media company. She has recently been appointed to the board and, as Chief Digital Officer (CDO), is responsible for initiating the company's digital transformation. Prior to this, she enjoyed a very successful period as the company's IT director. Stories like Lucy's are an exception, since women working in IT roles are still massively outnumbered by men. Lucy arrived at her current role in a roundabout way: having studied mathematics, she began her career in an IT consultancy before moving to her current organization. She has now been here for seven years and has built a stellar career. Lucy is ambitious and considered an expert in technology and digitalization.

The role Lucy has taken on is a demanding one. Digitalization is driving wholesale disruption across the media industry, and many companies are in a state of radical change. This change goes far beyond the technical aspects. While efficiency, planning, and established formats were once the formula for media success, the focus has now shifted to flexibility, speed, and reimagination. Hierarchies and the strict division of labor are being usurped by collaboration, empowerment, and co-creation. Lucy's job is both to drive technical change and to bring about a mindset shift among employees.

Lucy has found the transition to her new role challenging. For one thing, she is getting used to her newfound responsibility for the company's strategy; for another, she continues to be drawn into the minutiae of her previous role as IT director, waylaid by day-to-day issues with the IT infrastructure. Our coaching sessions focus on helping Lucy adjust to her recent promotion to the board. She has a new role on paper; how can she begin to embrace this role mentally, too?

Embracing and Accepting Oneself in a New Role

"How was last week's board meeting?" I ask. "You wanted to present some parts of the new digital strategy, right?"

"It was frustrating," comes the reply. "I only had thirty minutes, so there wasn't even time to talk about the strategy—just the tech requirements and the budget. To be honest, I got the impression that my colleagues weren't taking it that seriously anyway. They seemed more interested in complaining about the problems with the new IT infrastructure."

"But you're not responsible for that anymore, are you?" I ask. "I thought that was organized differently now."

"People seem to think that I am. My team and I have taken care of all the IT issues here over the last three years. I think we managed to achieve a lot–that's why I'm known as Wonder Woman. The problem is that the label has stuck. Once Wonder Woman, always Wonder Woman. It's no surprise that some of them find it strange to suddenly hear me talking strategy." Her tone becomes sarcastic. "To be honest, I was just glad that no one stopped the meeting to ask me to set up their laptop."

"And when you look at yourself, do you see a CDO?" I ask. "Or are you still mentally in your old role?"

"I have to admit, I haven't quite made the jump in my head. It's hard for me to let go. It's like a reflex. I keep finding myself dealing with issues that shouldn't be mine to deal with anymore." Her tone is now more thoughtful.

"Well, if *you* haven't let go of your old role, it's hardly going to be possible to change your colleagues' perception."

"That much is clear," she says with conviction, addressing herself more than me. "I need to *fix* that misperception, and fast."

"*Fixing*," I reply. "That sounds more like an IT director speaking than a strategist."

"So, what should I do, then?"

"Maybe you should try looking at things through a new lens. Try to see things less from the perspective of an IT manager–from the perspective of needing a definitive fix–and more from the strategic point of view of a CDO, in keeping with your new identity. You can start by asking yourself the right questions."

"Which would be . . .?"

"Well, for example: What do your colleagues have to gain from supporting you in your new role as CDO?"

She pauses briefly. "I suspect they're all driven by very different interests. Some–our CEO, for example–are willing to support me because their personal success depends on the success of the groupwide digital transformation. Other people's interests are more tactical. They're more concerned with how digitalization could work in their own area of responsibility."

"And how is your relationship with your colleagues?" I probe.

"Again, it varies from person to person. Some people display an active interaction style and proactively reach out to me. Our CEO is one of them. Other people seem more passive and don't take the initiative in relationship building."

"Great," I say. "I think we have a good basis for action."

Leaving the Comfort Zone

We develop a stakeholder matrix. First, we divide Lucy's board and managerial colleagues into two categories based on their interaction focus. The first is those whose interest in digitalization is more tactical and self-serving—those primarily seeking to optimize their own area of responsibility, for example. The second is those who support Lucy's digital strategy without conditions or caveats.

We then divide each group into two subgroups based on their interaction style: those with an active style, who proactively reach out to Lucy, and those with a passive style, with whom she has to take the initiative. We then develop four tailored plans—one for each subgroup—aimed at helping Lucy win support for her ideas.

"I must admit, up until now, I've tended to categorize my colleagues according to the urgency of their IT needs," she laughs. "I'm beginning to understand what you mean when you talk about a strategic board perspective."

"How soon will you have a chance to talk about the digitalization strategy?" I ask.

"Our next scheduled board meeting is in two weeks. We'll be focusing on the digital strategy and all the questions around it."

"And how far have you gotten with your preparation?"

"It's going well," she replies proudly. "My team is preparing a big presentation—there'll be at least fifty slides. We're going to make sure that every question is answered."

"Mightn't that just leave your listeners cold?" My question is deliberately provocative, and Lucy is taken aback.

"What do you mean?!"

"To me, fifty slides sounds like an IT process description, not a strategy presentation."

"Perhaps you're right," she says quietly. "That might be the IT manager in me rearing its head again. But how else am I supposed to explain all the details we've planned?"

"Well, do you actually need to? What's your goal for the meeting? What are you actually trying to achieve?"

"I want to create a spirit of optimism and confidence in our strategy. At the end of the day, we're trying to reinvent the digital media experience for our customers. We have the potential to become a kind of Netflix in our segment. I really believe this strategy is going to take us places." As she says this, I can feel her enthusiasm from the other end of the videoconference. I almost feel like joining her team myself.

"That's a very powerful strategic narrative," I say. "Why don't you tell this story instead of boring the board with the technical stuff? I think the answer lies in getting out of your comfort zone."

"What do you mean?" Lucy says. "I mean, practically?"

"Well," I say, "what would happen if you had five slides instead fifty, if you started off by simply explaining where you want to go? What if you asked questions instead of having all the answers? What if you walked into the meeting as a CDO, not an IT director, and explained your vision by addressing your colleagues as equals?"

Lucy thinks for a moment, then answers. "That would mean letting go of my old role in my head, not just on paper, and starting to view myself as a CDO." She pauses again, then continues: "I get what you mean about leaving my comfort zone, but I don't think it will be easy. I think it will require a lot of courage."

Growing into a New Role

For the next two weeks, Lucy prepares intensively for the upcoming board meeting. She uses the stakeholder matrix to anticipate possible reactions and holds initial talks with individual board colleagues. She seeks the advice of former colleagues—two in particular—who occupy similar board positions at other companies and have acquired experience with extensive digital transformation programs. This helps her to make her vision crisper, sharper, and more tangible. Prior to the meeting, she sends her colleagues an inspiring article on digital business transformation to get everyone fired up.

A Meeting to Remember

Our next coaching session takes place two days after the meeting. I dial in on time, but Lucy isn't there. This isn't like her at all. To my surprise, I find her calling my cell phone.

"Sorry—I couldn't connect. I'm having problems with my computer. Can we speak the old-fashioned way today?"

"Of course. How was the meeting?" I am keen to know.

"It was fantastic!" she begins. "It was the first time in a long time that the executive team had met in person. All of us were pleased to be there; the mood at the start was really good. To be honest, yes, I did have cold feet, and I brought my fifty slides as backup. But I didn't need them. I presented six slides explaining my vision, then we got straight into talking about how we could tackle the transformation as a company and what resources we would need. We ended with some really great ideas. We could barely stop the CFO once he got going: he was up and standing at the flipchart himself. I've never seen anything like it. In the end, all my proposals for the digital strategy were approved, and my colleagues pledged their full support."

"Congratulations!" I say. "Honestly, I never doubted for a moment that you were going to do brilliantly. There's one thing I'm still worried about, though."

"What's that?!"

"Your malfunctioning computer, of course!" I try to keep as straight a face as possible.

Lucy laughs down the telephone. "It might seem hard to believe, but I've completely forgotten how to fix things these last few weeks. It all feels rather far away all of a sudden."

"It sounds like you've cast off the ropes, as it were," I say. "Your CDO journey can now begin."

"I feel like I'm already out of the harbor," Lucy says, laughing.

What We Can Learn from Lucy

▶ *To adapt to a new role, we must leave behind behavioral patterns that previously brought us success.*

Lucy had two challenges to overcome. First, she had to make the mental leap from her previous role as IT director to her new role on the board. This required her to let go of much of what had made her successful thus far–the behaviors that had helped her make it to the board in the first place. The paradox was clear. Lucy's second challenge was to fundamentally transform her relationships with colleagues on the board, who had become accustomed to viewing her as an IT service provider. All at once, she was at the forefront of the company's strategy. To be accepted in her new role, she had to find a way to shed her old image. In my experience, this step is one of the most challenging of all.

▶ *To fully assert ourselves in a new role, we must win the support of those around us.*
Lucy needed the full support of the executive team for the digital transformation. To simply ask for this support would have been naive. For one thing, the interests of various colleagues in the matter were too disparate; for another, her personal relationships were not yet established enough. For this reason, we began by defining the various groups of stakeholders in order to get a clear picture of their motives. Next, we developed tailored tactics for dealing with each group to increase the chances of influencing them. In addition, Lucy cleverly used the time before the meeting to "prewire" the digital strategy in bilateral talks, collect best-practice examples, and generate interest for the subject among the board.

▶ *Breaking old habits sometimes requires active unlearning.*
When it came to preparing her presentation, Lucy initially defaulted to what she knew from her former role as an IT expert. Though she had a strong strategic story to tell, she was tempted to hide behind technical details; this was the terrain on which she felt safe. To achieve her goals, she had to be prepared to walk into the meeting and relinquish that familiar sense of safety. This was necessary not only to convince the team of her ideas, but to win acceptance for herself on a personal level. Though she didn't need it, the fifty-slide presentation in her pocket acted as an invisible safety net, giving her the courage to step out of her comfort zone. By the end of the meeting, she had not only gained approval for the digital strategy, but also made the mental transition to her role on the board.

Keep reading to the end of the chapter to find out where Lucy is now.

On Adaptation, Actively Unlearning, and Asserting Oneself in a New Role

Climbing the career ladder demands the ability to adapt and readapt many times over. This is because the rules for success change with every step. This adage holds just as true for internal promotion within a company as for lateral entry into another one. To assert ourselves in a new role, first we must let go of the old one—and with it, formulas for success that are no longer conducive to our goals. This is the only way to make room for something new. Often, this can require a conscious process of unlearning: an active forgetting of skills and knowledge that might have served us well in the past. The following section explains how to go about this.

Adaptation: Why Old Formulas for Success Suddenly Cease to Function

"It is not the strongest of the species that survives, nor the most intelligent. It is the one that is most adaptable to change." You're no doubt familiar with this quote—commonly attributed to Charles Darwin, though unlikely his exact words—on the evolution of species. This biological principle can be transferred neatly to the business world. As studies show, adaptability is one of the most important skills that leaders must master.

Adaptability: An Evergreen Factor for Success

More than twenty-five years ago, a study by the Center for Creative Leadership revealed the importance of adaptability for advancing up the career ladder. The study examined enduring success factors for European and US leaders, independent of the cultural context (Leslie and van Velsor 1996). It contrasted managers who had made it to the top with those who hadn't been so successful, because they either left their companies involuntarily or remained but weren't promoted further. The study made an important contribution to our understanding of success in senior leadership positions.

Remove: Discarding Behaviors That No Longer Benefit Us

Among other things, it defined the ability to develop and adapt as a key success factor for executives.

A recent study by Boston Consulting Group (BCG) backed up this finding. A survey of over five thousand managers and employees in Germany, China, France, Great Britain, and the US identified the special qualities that successful managers must possess in the "new normal" (Boston Consulting Group 2019). In addition to empathy and the abilities to develop teams, demonstrate consideration, and listen—all qualities that are particularly important in times of virtual leadership—the findings also included the importance of adaptability. Leaders must be able to adapt to new situations and to manage uncertainty in the business environment. Unexpected and unknowable "black swan" events such as the pandemic and the Ukraine war, which affect the course of business despite best-laid plans, underscore this need.

The Grow-or-Go Principle: Adaptation in Practice— A Consulting Case Study

Adaptability is most required when one is taking on a new task or responsibility. This is perhaps best demonstrated by an analogy from the world of sports. If a short-distance sprinter tries their hand at a marathon, they'll need to adapt their running technique or else quickly face overexertion. The career ladder is no different. Here, I speak from personal experience.

The principle of adaptation in management consultancies is often referred to as "grow or go." In addition to my own client projects, for many years I was responsible for the internal development of consultants at my firm. I was privileged to support many of them on their way to becoming senior partners. Adaptability is especially important for careers in consultancy, since those who fail to reach the next rung of the ladder have no choice but to leave. Of course, for those consultants who wish to switch paths after three to five years anyway, adaptability isn't quite so crucial. These people might, for example, go on to start their own company or move to a senior position with a client. But those who want to progress to partner must keep adapting at each new stage—just like a chameleon changes color and yet remains its essential self.

"Sorry, I'm New Here": Why Lateral Movers Often Struggle to Adapt

Many of you have probably been approached by a recruiter to talk about an attractive role. Suddenly, the opportunity for the long-awaited leap to senior executive or board member flashes before your eyes. Perhaps you even have a chance at the top job. The move is presented as a once-in-a-lifetime opportunity to continue advancing your career elsewhere. As tempting as they may sound on the surface, such situations call for caution. Ultimately, a lateral move can often feel like jumping from one moving train to the next, especially if the jump is at the upper echelons of management. Inevitably, some people end up landing on the tracks. In this case, too, adaptability is needed.

Harvard professor Boris Groysberg investigated this phenomenon by looking at the careers of analysts in investment banks. Many banks seek out external talent—candidates who have demonstrated outstanding performance and built impressive track records—in their efforts to remain competitive. Accordingly, it's not uncommon for these new hires to enter their roles amidst a great deal of hype and anticipatory plaudits. What Groysberg found was that many of these star analysts and high-potential hires suffered an immediate and lasting decline in performance (Groysberg 2012). For one reason or another, they were unable to perform at their previous level upon entering the new environment. Many proved to have been far more dependent on the proprietary resources, networks, and organizational cultures of their previous workplaces than they realized. They failed to adapt to the changed environment.

This is not only the case with investment banks. In my time as a recruiting director in consulting, I saw numerous talented lateral hires—individuals with impressive CVs and demonstrable successes—who failed, contrary to all expectations. The cases I see as a coach reveal a similar pattern. From heads of sales to members of the board, there are various promising lateral moves that simply do not work out in practice. The reason is almost always along the same lines: a lack of ability to adapt to the new environment.

When it comes to advancing one's career, adaptability is likely to be even more important in the future than it is today. Statistics show that successive generations are changing jobs with increasing frequency. Some 91 percent of millennials, the generation born between 1977 and

1997, are expected to have fifteen to twenty jobs during their working lives (Meister 2012). For this generation, the ability to quickly and effectively transition and adapt to a new role is becoming a key professional competency (Meister 2012).

Caution: Trip Hazard!

Personal adaptability is also required in the event of organizational changes such as restructuring or takeovers, where new tasks are to be taken on or areas of responsibility suddenly relinquished. Not everyone finds it easy to cope with these experiences, which—admittedly—can be painful. The fact remains, though, that those who are unable to grow flexibly within a new structure can quickly find themselves out of a job. In one case, I witnessed a sales manager stubbornly refuse to adjust to a new structure following reorganization. He buried his head in the sand and continued to use his informal network to "manage" areas for which he was no longer responsible. After repeated inevitable conflicts, the company eventually let him go.

Similarly, leaders who remain successful over time have certain qualities in common. When appointed to a new leadership role, these leaders are able to grow and evolve beyond their previous limits instead of coming up against them. Not everyone is able to do this. In his bestseller *The Crucial 90 Days*, author and leadership expert Michael Watkins describes how a lack of adaptability is one of the most common reasons for careers to fail (Watkins 2014). When the transition to a new role goes awry, he wrote, there's usually one of two reasons at play: either the essential demands of the new role haven't been understood, or the ability and flexibility to adapt to them are lacking. But why does this happen? What's the secret of adaptability?

Why We Find It So Difficult to Adapt

Adaptation is inherently paradoxical. When successful people move up the ladder, they assume they must continue the behaviors that have brought them success thus far. Perhaps they should even do more of them! While they're willing to add new skills to their toolbox, they won't give up what they know. They certainly won't be willing to abandon their proven habits and principles for success. Unfortunately, it's often this exact form of adaptation that is required for success in a new role. The paradox is clear. *How can something that has brought me so far be getting me nowhere now?* they wonder. Even worse, in the new situation, these established habits and principles may not be merely ineffective but actively detrimental. This is a hard problem to tackle.

US author Marshall Goldsmith addresses this issue in depth in his best-selling book *What Got You Here Won't Get You There* (Goldsmith 2007). He lists a number of destructive habits and behaviors that readers may have found tactically useful in the past but are guaranteed to become problematic over time. These include:

- the need to win at all costs;
- the overwhelming desire to be heard in every conversation;
- passing judgment;
- making destructive comments;
- the need to share negative thoughts, even when they're not asked for;
- withholding information;
- overestimating one's contributions;
- the need to be seen as smart by the world;
- the inability to give proper recognition;
- passing the buck;
- refusing to admit being wrong;
- an unwillingness to listen; and
- an excessive need to be "me"—even if that involves hurting others.

Importantly, it's not only destructive behavior but also an overreliance on one's known strengths that can become an issue in a new role. "To a man with a hammer, everything looks like a nail," Mark Twain is said to have written. Accordingly, if a new job isn't going as planned, we have two possible courses of action. The first is to recognize that this new role requires something different from what we've been doing thus far. Armed with this insight, we initiate a change of course and cultivate a willingness to leave the past behind. This approach will likely be fruitful. In the second, less preferable course of action, we refuse to recognize the need to adapt and doggedly default to our established strengths. We not only continue what we're already doing, but up the ante, too. Sadly, this approach rarely yields results. In the worst-case scenario, we drive ourselves and others to burnout.

Consider the fictional example of an analyst known for his excellent analytical skills. He is promoted to the role of project manager and takes on leadership responsibilities. Instead of embracing his leadership role, developing his team members, and attempting to make them into outstanding analysts after his own example, he continues to rely on his analytical skills alone. He gatekeeps every important analysis for himself in order to prove that he can excel at it. His team feels frustrated and increasingly neglected. Gradually, the analyst becomes a bottleneck, and eventually he fails at the job completely. Utterly demotivated, he leaves the company.

Exercise: How Have You Adapted in the Past?

Reflect on the following questions:

- Which of your personal principles have played a pivotal role in your success in the past?
- Which of your principles of success have you had to leave behind? Why?
- Which of your principles of success might you have to leave behind in order to continue developing in the future?

As for how we can adapt successfully, sometimes we have to free up space in our heads first.

Actively Unlearning: The Art of the Mental Declutter

There is a famous story in which a scientist visits a Zen master in order to learn more about Zen. The Zen master offers his guest tea. While the scientist speaks without drawing breath and expounds his own theory on the subject, the Zen master continues to pour from the pot. Eventually, the cup overflows. "What are you doing?" the scientist exclaims, horrified. "You're spilling it everywhere!"

"You can't pour tea into a full cup," comes the Zen master's calm reply.

Bidding Farewell to Old Ways of Thinking

Our heads are full to the brim with information. We have no spare capacity for absorbing new things and, as a result, no capacity for being open to changes either. From time to time, therefore, it can be worthwhile to examine the "expiration date" of our accumulated knowledge and to clear out and dispose of what no longer serves us. If something is no longer valuable or helpful—or if it has become an active hindrance—it has to go. Moreover, just like when changing the oil in a car, we must first drain the old oil before adding the new. In other words: we must get rid of old beliefs and thought patterns before we can take on new information.

Never was this more evident to me than when I moved into consulting as a lateral hire. Compared to the graduates straight from university, who functioned as blank "hard drives" in terms of their capacity to absorb information, it took me considerably longer to settle in and to acquire new methods and skills. This had less to do with a lack of understanding than with my need to part with old ways of thinking: to clear space on my hard drive for learning new things. This was why, as a lateral hire, my learning curve was somewhat flatter at first than that of the graduates I worked alongside.

"You Have to 'Unlearn'": How We Can Go About Creating Space in Our Heads

How do we go about creating space in our heads? "We spend a lot of time teaching leaders what to do. We don't spend enough time teaching leaders what to stop," Peter Drucker is quoted as saying (Goldsmith 2007). Indeed, there's an almost overwhelming array of training courses aimed at teaching managers new methods. Training providers' databases range from popular courses like Agile Leadership to rather more eclectic-sounding offerings like Leading with Zen. Unfortunately, participants rarely learn what they need to stop doing. It's rarer still that they learn to do this effectively.

"You have to 'unlearn,' you have to forget what you know. You have to be able to separate yourself from it," said Dutch writer Harry Mulisch (Mulisch and Saalbach 1999). The term *unlearning* is one I find highly apt. By placing the emphasis on the active process, it cuts to the essence of what is required: actively disengaging from one's old habits and accepted ideas in order to create room in one's mind. Framed as the opposite of learning, it slots neatly into the inner dialogue governing personal processes of change. This dialogue is characterized by opposites:

- renew yet preserve;
- leave yet stay;
- analyze yet also feel; and
- learn and simultaneously unlearn.

Unlearning is especially important when old habits and beliefs aren't compatible with the new identity and environment. Consider, for instance, the real-life example of a corporate financial controller who moved to a CFO role in a medium-size company and recognized that his management style didn't fit his new place of work. In his old company, he had cultivated something of a drill sergeant mentality and a belief that teams "had to be tightly run," as he said. Whenever a hint of discontent began to bubble, he reflexively cracked down. This stood in stark contrast to the culture of the new company, which was characterized by listening, team spirit, and a high degree of freedom and autonomy. After only a short time, the first employees in his team began to quit. But because the manager remained perceptive to the consequences of his behavior, he gradually succeeded in discarding the harshness of his old methods and adapting to the culture of his new employer. He unlearned.

Depending on the new environment, there may be a variety of behavior patterns that need to be unlearned. These could include:

- thinking based on hierarchies or departmental boundaries;
- an excessive focus on adherence to rules;
- a tendency to press ahead without sufficient planning;
- strong emotional reactions;
- the reflexive urge to go on the defensive;
- the compulsion to give an opinion, even when one has nothing to say;
- unconscious bias; and
- the conviction that one is always in the right.

> Unlearning means stopping such behavior and discarding the patterns of thinking that underpin it.

The *Columbia* Disaster: When Unlearning Becomes Vital for Survival

One of the most interesting encounters of my professional career was with the former US astronaut Eileen Collins: the first woman to pilot a space shuttle. A conference in Texas brought me the privileged opportunity to talk to Eileen in person. She told me about the *Columbia* disaster of 2003 and the subsequent investigation into its cause. Tragically, the *Columbia* space shuttle had broken apart on reentry into the Earth's atmosphere, killing all seven crew members. The reason? A piece of insulative foam had come away from the shuttle's external tank and torn a hole in the thermal protection shield. Though the issue of the detaching foam had long been known from previous missions, engineers considered it a tolerable problem because it hadn't caused any damage thus far. NASA and its leaders were forced to break with a stance they had previously deemed acceptable. Its leaders had to "collectively unlearn," as Eileen said.

Getting Rid of Troublesome Habits: Unlearning in Practice

When we struggle to disengage from old patterns of thinking and acting, it is often because we are stuck in "run mode." We're unable to see our own problem. This is precisely when it's important to pause, think, and reflect, since only by becoming aware of our habits and behaviors can we even begin to think about stopping them. One way to do this is by keeping a daily journal and reflecting regularly on targeted questions. The so-called KEEP-STOP-START logic has proven a useful approach in practice. Ask yourself:

- What should I KEEP?
- What should I STOP?
- What should I START?

Exercise: Journaling

Take ten minutes each evening to reflect on the past day, then answer the following three questions:

1. KEEP: Which of my habits and behaviors have helped me today?
2. STOP: Which of my habits and behaviors have hindered me today?
3. START: What new habits and behaviors might have been useful to me?

Make this exercise part of your daily routine. You'll be surprised at the insights you discover.

Becoming aware is an important first step, but not the destination. The problem with old habits and behaviors is that it's not so simple to set them aside. In technical language, they take on an inertia; once they're set in motion, it takes strength to stop them again. What makes things harder still is that these old behaviors function like reflexes. Before we're aware of it, we've said or done something we didn't consciously intend to. The reflex happens very quickly. A meditation teacher once told me: "You have about half a second to react."

The Elephant and the Rider

Clearly, resolving to stop a behavior at the rational level is not sufficient to bring about the desired result. In psychology, this concept is illustrated by the analogy of the elephant and the rider (Haidt 2006). The rider represents the rational, conscious side of our mind; the elephant, our emotional and automatic reactions. These automatic processes make it easier for us to exist from day to day, since we have neither the time nor the capacity to think through every decision from scratch. The problem arises when the elephant's plans diverge from our rational intentions. When this occurs, the elephant goes the way it wants; we can only passively observe the outcome in frustration. These automatic processes are spontaneous and involuntary. To make things trickier still, we're unaware of them in the moment and can recognize them only from the result. The elephant follows an inner instinct for preservation and is satisfied whenever it takes a step toward its goal.

For change to occur, both rider and elephant must act in unison. The key to this lies in connecting with our emotions. Only by doing so can we persuade the elephant, the emotional side of the brain, to break into a trot. If we want to appeal to the elephant, we must replace the pattern of analyze-think-change with see-feel-change, as authors Fred (Chip) Heath and Jeffrey (Dan) Heath wrote in their bestseller *Switch* (Heath and Heath 2013).

We need an image in our minds of where we want to be, one that provides an emotional incentive for stopping our existing behaviors and habits.

In the case of the *Columbia* disaster, it was the NASA engineers' fear of a repeat tragedy that led to rethinking and unlearning. In the wider world, too, many of us become open to change only as a result of a negative experience. There are numerous examples of leaders, including CEOs, who were required to fail professionally first in order to understand what they needed to alter.

But it's not only negative feelings that can effect a change in thinking. Those who succeed in creating an association between unlearning and positive emotions will be well equipped to expand their repertoires as leaders. If a leader is able to witness firsthand how employees flourish and become more productive as a result of feeling less criticized, that leader will automatically begin to restrain their criticism. Not only this, but they'll readily experiment with a new approach to leadership in other aspects of their role as well. If, by contrast, a leader fails to internalize this positive association and merely resolves rationally to criticize less—in the hopes of polishing their own image, for example—they'll find it difficult to steer the elephant in the right direction at critical moments. They're very likely to "relapse" repeatedly and go back to criticizing again.

Remove: Discarding Behaviors That No Longer Benefit Us

Unlearning is a key skill that frees us from the habits and behaviors that hold us back. Once we've done this, we will be mentally prepared to assert ourselves in a new role.

Asserting Oneself in a New Role: How to Make a Success of a New Job

The ink on the employment contract is dry, the champagne has been drunk, and the congratulatory emails have been opened. There is nothing left but for the new job to begin. Yet there's still a mental transition to be tackled—and as I know from harsh experience, the difficulty of this isn't to be underestimated.

Transitioning to a New Role: A Real-Life Case Study

As I transitioned from each of my professional roles to the next, there were several occasions on which I had to concede that the journey wasn't quite as simple as I had expected. Since this book is also about looking inside one's own "engine compartment," I'll use the example of myself—specifically, my move from engineering to management consulting—to illustrate the transition process. I was full of anticipation for my new adventure, almost like the feeling you get when counting down to a vacation on a beautiful island. Unfortunately, no one had warned me that the crossing would be very stormy indeed.

Cast Off! The Crossing Begins

In my very first weeks of consulting, I realized I was dealing with a wholly different world. I had spent eight years in an industrial group with a corporate headquarters and fixed structures. Not only had this provided me with a clear sense of orientation, but I had also unconsciously learned to think in an exclusively vertical and hierarchical fashion. In management consulting, things were quite different: I found a laterally networked organization with numerous offices and topic-specific teams. Decisions were made within hours, not weeks, as I was used to. In order to be successful, I had to network horizontally with colleagues from different areas. I had a hard time adjusting to that at first.

Worse still, it was only now that it became truly apparent to me that I would need to prove myself all over again. At my old job, I had earned a favorable internal reputation and a great deal of trust in my abilities—up to and among the board members—that was grounded in a yearslong series of successes. It was like a bank account I had paid into over time, with the additional rewards of self-confidence and a psychological sense of security. In my new environment, nobody knew who I was. I had left my track record behind, so to speak, and my reputation balance was back to zero. That was a frightening realization. My first task was to learn to live without the security and sense of orientation I was used to. To do that, I had to mentally relinquish both. In this regard, the pride and elation of my acceptance to such a renowned consultancy helped me a little along the way.

En Route on a Stormy Sea

Sadly, this brief feeling of positivity dissipated quickly in the next phase. I had gone into consulting because I wanted to learn things, but I had underestimated how much I had to learn. At my previous job, I had analyzed markets, introduced lean production processes, presented at numerous management conferences, and received a great deal of applause for all. Here, I was forced to take one criticism after another. My analyses were not well founded enough, the "So what?" was missing from my slides, and my presentations had no "storyline." Accordingly, my first review was distinctly mediocre. My hoped-for promotion to project leader after a year did not materialize.

This was a serious test for my ego. Increasingly, I began to doubt myself and even to consider whether my entire move—from an established position in an industrial group to the fast-paced world of consultancy—might have been a huge mistake. When my former boss called me, I briefly thought of returning to my old job. At the same time, there were moments in which I enjoyed the new environment: the relaxed atmosphere in the office, the stimulating conversations, the intellectual challenge, and the chance to work on corporate strategy, a topic I found hugely fascinating. I felt torn, as if tossed around between huge waves in the middle of the ocean.

The Arrival: Finally, Land in Sight

Eventually the waves subsided and I found myself on calmer seas. Dry land came into sight. Little by little, I was able to recognize the successes I had achieved in my consulting role thus far. I increasingly enjoyed my work and learned more every day. After a little longer than originally planned, I was promoted to project leader. From there on, things only got better. It was as though my previous chapter had closed and I had finally bid goodbye to my engineer's identity. For me, it was this mental farewell that truly marked the new beginning.

Quite unexpectedly, a few years later, a message arrived from my old world. It felt so distant that it may as well have been a postcard from across the ocean. It was the HR manager on the line: they wanted to discuss a position on the board. I was curious and flattered, so I accepted the invitation. No sooner had I entered the company parking lot—and long-faded memories had begun to surface—than I knew that I would not return. I turned down the offer. My transition to the new world was long since complete. A return would have meant a whole new "crossing," this time in the other direction. I didn't feel ready for it, and I never regretted the decision. I was elected partner shortly afterward.

The Three Phases of Transition

When we transition from one role and identity to the next, this process takes place in phases. My own journey comprised three phases. First, I had to mentally let go of the environment I knew. Next, I spent a period feeling adrift between the two worlds. Finally, sometime after taking up the role, I had a sense of having embarked upon my new beginning for real. It was a simultaneous feeling of letting go and arriving: experiences that occurred in two opposing waves.

When I later took on new management responsibilities and finally became a self-employed coach, I recognized aspects of the transition experience I had previously undergone. Never again, however, did I experience

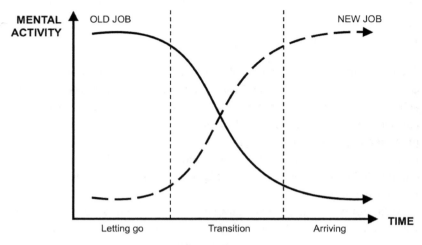

MENTAL ACTIVITY | OLD JOB | NEW JOB

TIME

Letting go | Transition | Arriving

The transition process

it with the same intensity. In their book *Managing Transitions*, American authors and organizational consultants William Bridges and Susan Bridges describe transition in a similar way. They, too, distinguish between three phases of the transition process (Bridges and Bridges 2018): "ending what currently is," the "neutral zone," and the "new beginning." They write of how the new beginning can succeed only if we end what we know and are ready to let go. Letting go is probably the hardest part of all.

Letting Go in Order to Move Forward

From my own experience and from numerous conversations with coaching clients, I know how difficult it can be to let go. For lateral and vertical career movers alike, letting go of old habits and "truths" can be a painful experience. In my work, I observe four areas in which career movers find letting go particularly difficult: letting go of old identities, letting go of the need for praise and recognition, letting go of trusted relationships, and letting go of old freedoms.

Remove: Discarding Behaviors That No Longer Benefit Us

Letting Go of Old Identities

A client of mine, an engineer, had once been responsible for Machine X. So synonymous was he with this machine that he became known internally as Mr. X. That was his identity, and he was proud of it. He knew every last detail of the product. When he later took over responsibility for an entire business unit, he became Mr. Business Unit instead. Machine X was now just one product of many for which he was responsible. For some time after assuming the role, he continued to fall back into his old identity and to concern himself primarily with matters regarding Machine X. This was perhaps not surprising: it was where he knew his way around and what he knew the best. Unfortunately, the new role very nearly meant the end of his career. What's interesting is that he's not an isolated case. The same thing happened to a sales manager who took over a business unit and a CFO who became CEO. All had been highly successful in their previous roles and, for that very reason, had a hard time letting go of their old identities. We saw the same with Lucy, too.

Letting Go of the Need for Praise and Recognition

Perfectionists, in particular, strive for praise and recognition. The problem is that praise creates a quasi–parent-child relationship. In transactional analysis, a communication model from psychology, the praiser is described as acting in the "Parent" ego state (Berne 2019). They are like a parent praising us for good grades at school. Those who seek praise—whether from colleagues, customers, or managers—render themselves small in the eyes of their counterparts. While they may appear perfectly professionally competent, they take on the aura of a nerd. This isn't compatible with the role of an authentic leader, who must act and react from the "Adult" ego state. When we rise to the upper echelons of management—as a board member or partner, if not before—it is therefore important to disengage from the need for praise and recognition. In effect, we must grow up. This necessarily requires us to let go.

A final but important note: praise isn't to be confused with appreciation, which by its nature always takes place in a spirit of mutual respect and equality.

Letting Go of Old Relationships

"As soon as I enter the room, colleagues' conversations fall silent," a client recounted, describing what had changed for him personally since his promotion to the executive board. "I'm no longer invited to gatherings outside work, either." Those who make it to the very top may experience transition in a particularly painful fashion. Relationships with former colleagues—perhaps even friends—will change, regardless of whether we want them to or not. As the saying goes: it's lonely at the top. Old relationships must be let go as the price for moving up the ladder.

Letting Go of Old Freedoms

A client of mine had taken on her first CEO position at a high-profile engineering company. In her first public interview, she discussed the possible exit of the company from an unprofitable part of the market. While it wasn't her first time talking on the subject, it *was* her first time doing so as CEO. She was unprepared for the vehemence of the reactions that met her, from the impact on the share price to the emotional responses. Those who rise to the top must not underestimate the increased weight of their words and deeds. While this impact can be positive, too—when delivered by a CEO, a few sincere words of appreciation can do more than an incentive trip to the Maldives—the fact remains that the pressure of the public gaze brings inevitable restrictions on personal freedoms. These are things we must mentally surrender.

Exercise: Coming to Grips with the Transition Process

Use the following questions the next time you find yourself in a period of transition.

Phase 1: Ending what currently is
- How do you personally feel about the change?
- Which old rules still apply? Which new rules must you now adhere to?

Phase 2: The neutral zone
- What would happen if you did *not* change?
- If the challenge you now face were a gift, what gift might it be?

Phase 3: The new beginning
- How might a successful day look in the future? What are you looking forward to?
- What new skills do you need?

The end of the transition process marks the new beginning. At this stage, those who have succeeded in letting go will be ready to take on new habits and experiment with new professional identities.

In a nutshell:

- If you want to be successful as a leader, you need to be able to develop and adapt as an individual.
- In order to adapt, paradoxically, you must be willing to part with what has made you successful thus far.
- To create space in your mind for new things, you must be capable of unlearning–again and again.
- Active unlearning helps you get rid of old habits and behaviors. You achieve it by gaining insight into the old behavior and creating an emotional incentive for the new one.
- The transition to a new leadership role typically takes place in three phases: ending what currently is, the neutral zone, and the new beginning. The transition can be challenging.
- To truly let go, you must also relinquish old habits and accepted truths. This part is often particularly difficult.

For the Curious among You: Where Lucy Is Now

Lucy has excelled at all aspects of her journey from IT expert to board member. She has experienced the aforementioned new beginning in her business role, learned a great deal, and gained self-confidence. She is accepted by all members of the executive team and has overseen her first successful pilot projects, which have earned her a high level of credibility in her role as Chief Digital Officer. Her own organizational area has grown significantly. Above all, she is highly skillful at involving other areas of the company in the digital transformation. In many respects, she is considered the guardian of the company's new digital focus.

MAINTENANCE MANUAL, PART II

REPLACE AND RESTART

Why Thinking Doesn't Always
Lead to Acting . . .
and Why You Might Want to Try
Things the Other Way Around

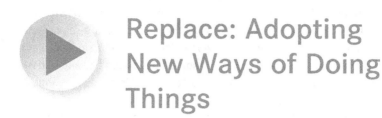

Replace: Adopting New Ways of Doing Things

Regular spark plug replacement is vital for the proper functioning of a car's engine.

−AUTOMOBILE MAGAZINE *AUTOBILD*, 2019

If a car is misfiring and the engine generally not running as it should, it might be time to change the spark plugs. In the same way, we must be open to periodic change if we want to keep our careers running smoothly. Old behaviors and skills must sometimes be replaced with new ones, especially if things aren't going well in the initial stages of a new job. The inability to adopt new behaviors and habits represents our fourth career stopper. On the other hand, those who are open to the cycle of learning and relearning will be able to access long-term success. Here is Jonas's story.

Case Study: Jonas

It's a rainy day at the beginning of March, and I'm meeting Jonas, a young partner from a renowned consultancy, for our very first coaching session. Jonas was elected partner around one year ago. As is customary with professional services firms, this appointment was the culmination of a long and grueling selection process. As a project leader, he was among the company's best, and he had built a reputation as a chemical industry expert. He was known for his probing questions, in-depth analysis, and specialist expertise. Now, as partner, he has assumed responsibility for a major client: ChemCo. His task is to systematically expand business with this client.

The Background

We sit in Jonas's tenth-floor office, looking out at the city view. Jonas appears tired and demotivated. "I think I'm in the wrong job," he begins. "When I was elected partner a year ago, it felt as though things were going really well. Since then, things have gone from bad to worse. I haven't sold a single project since I took over the ChemCo account. If something doesn't change soon, that's it for me here: I can start looking for a new job." He sounds anxious.

"Who's saying that?" I press him.

'Well, no one's actually saying it. I know how things go here, though."

"Okay. Let's start by imagining how things would be if they were going as hoped. Will you join me in a little thought experiment?"

"Sure," he replies curiously.

"Imagine a day exactly eight years from now. Picture yourself as a highly successfully partner: a person who is admired by others. It's a very special day. What are you seeing? What are you feeling? Describe it to me," I tell him.

Jonas gazes thoughtfully out the window. "I'm happy," he says. "We've helped to grow ChemCo significantly, which has made it one of our most important clients. On a personal level, the success has helped me to establish myself as partner—inside and outside the firm."

"A bit more specific, please," I probe. "Where exactly are you? What are you doing? Let your imagination run wild. What would be your dream?"

Jonas thinks for a moment. "I'm standing on a stage at a big company conference," he says. "But I'm not alone—the ChemCo CEO is with me. We're discussing the success of the ChemCo transformation. He's telling the audience how we as a consultancy have helped the company—what makes us different, why they wanted to work with us, what separates us from the rest." As he speaks, a little enthusiasm creeps back into his voice. His gaze brightens.

"A brilliant vision," I say. "And how *do* you differ from the competition? What does the ChemCo CEO have to say?"

"He says that we successfully anticipated ChemCo's challenges and proactively proposed a plan. At the same time, we're empathetic, we listen, we keep in touch, and we're honest about what we think—because we really want to help." Jonas delivers this message in a wholly compelling way.

"Perfect," I say. "Keep this image alive in your head. How did you get the ChemCo CEO to accept your invitation?"

"Well, probably by knowing him very well," Jonas replies. "I hope we'd be meeting regularly by then."

"And?"

"And because I've learned to sell—not only small projects, but big programs—directly to the board." There is light in Jonas's eyes.

"You're a proper rainmaker, then?" I ask. "You know, one of those partners who brings in all the business?"

"That would be my long-term dream," says Jonas. Then, somewhat shyly: "But I don't know if I have what it takes."

"Well, at the moment we're assuming you do," I say. "To me, your description indicates someone who not only *can* sell, but loves selling. How often do you meet the ChemCo CEO at the moment?"

"To be honest," he says, a little embarrassed, "I've only met him once."

"And who else do you meet from ChemCo?"

"My meetings tend to come about rather sporadically. It's not easy to make appointments with ChemCo, so we're focusing for now on a market study for the chemical sector. As soon as we have the findings, we'll try to get an appointment to present them."

"That sounds less like a rainmaker speaking than an analyst," I say. My question is deliberately somewhat provocative.

"What do you mean?" comes the surprised reply.

"You're continuing to do what you know you're good at: analyzing markets. If you want to become a rainmaker, you have to practice rainmaking. You've told me you want to meet this client regularly in the future and to start selling larger consulting programs. How many hours a week do you spend working on your client relationships, actually learning how to sell?"

"Probably too few," he replies. "Probably not even an hour a week."

"Maybe it's time to change that," I encourage him. "Maybe it's time to get into new habits."

"Which should be?" he asks curiously.

"Well, what do rainmakers spend their days doing?" I ask.

Jonas thinks for a moment, then answers. "They're constantly in touch with their clients, I suppose. They keep a list of hot leads—issues with the potential to turn into projects—and they keep at it, come what may."

"Then I believe we have plenty to go on," I say.

Anchoring New Behaviors

Together we develop a plan. Jonas creates a list of his most important ChemCo contacts, then evaluates each contact in light of two questions. First, he assesses the contact's influence over purchasing decisions; second, he assesses the closeness of the relationship, or how quickly he can set up an appointment. This allows Jonas to prioritize his contacts in a targeted way and to set goals for expanding his network. From the results, we whittle down the ten most important contacts. Jonas resolves to stay in touch with each of them and writes the next planned action beside each name.

In the next step, he creates a list with all of the ChemCo leads or topics that currently have the potential to become new projects. He divides these topics into four categories: those that are initial ideas, those he has previously discussed with ChemCo, those for which he has drafted an offer, and those for which he is currently in active negotiations. By doing this, he gets a good feel for his prospects of success as a partner in the coming year.

To supplement these steps, Jonas begins blocking off thirty minutes in his calendar each week. This time is reserved for planning concrete actions: telephone calls, videoconferences, or lunches with important ChemCo contacts in the following week. He seeks to establish small but regular business development activities as part of his regular working practices. As well as asking his assistant to remind him of this plan, Jonas agrees that she should work autonomously to set up additional appointments. In the months that follow, he works to implement the plan step-by-step. In our coaching sessions, we continue to discuss and monitor the status of the plan along with any necessary course corrections. Eventually, after a long break, we come together on a sunny December day for our final session.

Using the Flywheel Effect

"How's it going with ChemCo?" I immediately want to know.

Jonas smiles, the sun from the window hitting his face. He is full of vitality, completely different than when I first saw him. "I'd never have thought that setting new habits would create such a ripple effect," he says. "It's like we've started a flywheel that can't be stopped. We're getting more appointments all the time, including with the CEO. I've learned a lot about ChemCo, and I've really grown to care about it. It's like being in a real relationship—butterflies in the stomach and all." Then, more mysteriously: "We even said our 'I dos' last Friday."

"What do you mean?" I ask with interest.

He explains, "The ChemCo CEO gave us the go-ahead for an important project: working on the company's corporate strategy for the next five years. It could be the start of something really huge." He smiles proudly, then continues. "And it's not just a big deal for the team and for me—it's also a milestone for the consultancy. It's the first time we've supported ChemCo with its central corporate strategy."

"Congratulations!" I exclaim. "Maybe, in a few years, you'll be speaking to the CEO on stage at an internal conference. I don't know; I have a funny feeling."

"It's very possible," Jonas says, laughing.

What We Can Learn from Jonas

▶ *A powerful vision creates a positive state of mind.*

Jonas had failed to meet his high expectations of himself during his first year as partner. This triggered intense stress and fears of losing all he had worked for. For this reason, it was important, as a first step, to get Jonas back to a positive state of mind. He achieved this by engaging actively with his long-term dreams and his vision of becoming a rainmaker. Through this process, he was able to recognize that simply continuing the things he was good at wouldn't bring him success in his partner role. Incisive market analyses had gotten him noticed in the past. Now, as partner, he would be measured by his ability to build relationships and sell projects. To do this, he needed new habits and skills.

▶ *Career jumps entail vital behavior change.*

Jonas began by developing a concrete action plan for expanding his network of contacts at ChemCo and increasing his chances of selling future projects. Once he recognized that he had the tools to become successful, his nebulous fear of failure disappeared. Most importantly, however, he used his vision to develop a tailored learning program that would help him acquire new habits and skills. Without this learning program—that is, with the customer action plan alone—he would likely not have been so successful.

▶ *Rhythm and vibration are powerful tools in effecting change.*

When it came to his business development activities, Jonas made the conscious decision to take small but regular steps. This steady rhythm led to a stream of small successes with a self-reinforcing and motivating effect. Jonas succeeded in raising his positive vibrations: a crucial factor for his success. He kept this rhythm by asking his assistant to remind him of his plan. In psychology, this is referred to as a "nudge."

Keep reading to the end of the chapter to find out where Jonas is now.

On Vision, Vital Behavior Change, and Vibration

Those who wish to develop as leaders need a powerful vision to provide direction. They require new habits and behaviors to help them master the challenges of their new role. Finally, they need a system to set the personal change process into vibration. This vibration is what will sustain the personal change over time.

Vision: Stop Ruminating, Start Dreaming

"If you want to build a ship, don't drum up the men to gather wood, divide the work, and give orders. Instead, teach them to yearn for the vast and endless sea." Perhaps you're familiar with this well-known quote from French writer Antoine de Saint-Exupéry (*The Citadel*). If we seek to develop as people and become master architects in a particular field, longing and dreams play an important role. We need a powerful personal vision for the future before we can think about the practical change. To create this vision, we must first understand what motivates and drives us.

"Inside the Engine Compartment": Our Drivers and Motivators

For almost ten years at my previous consulting firm, I shared responsibility for recruiting in Germany. I conducted over one thousand interviews with young graduates during that time. For most of them, making the jump to a renowned consultancy would have represented the fulfillment of a lifelong dream. To each of them, I posed the same question: "Why do you want to work in consulting?" A tiny number—fewer than ten candidates—described being attracted by the job itself, the prospect of advising others. Salary played a similarly subordinate role. Almost all of them explained their ambition in terms of the desire to learn and make a difference.

To be happy and satisfied, we need to find meaning in our work and to know why we do it. There is a diverse range of motives that can serve as the source. The desire to learn new things and to make a difference is an example of an *intrinsic motive*. Intrinsic motives also include, for example, the opportunity to use our talents or to pursue our personal passions. Existing alongside these are *extrinsic motives*, such as salary and professional status.

Experience shows that high income and professional status do not lead to deep and long-lasting fulfillment. Of course, money provides financial freedom, and status is a source of pride. Yet the satisfaction these extrinsic motives bring doesn't last. No matter how high the salary or how lofty the status, we quickly get used to it. When a colleague receives a bigger bonus or is promoted more quickly than us, we're quick to feel dissatisfied and to want even more. This spiral is self-perpetuating. As a result, any attempt to seek genuine fulfillment and lasting happiness through money and status is a fool's errand.

Similarly, professional success alone cannot bring enduring happiness. By tethering our happiness solely to our professional achievements, we are vulnerable to being thrown off course by every minor failure. In reality, the formula is the other way around.

If we are happy, we have achieved the most important prerequisite for also being successful.

"Why?!"; or, In Search of Our Personal Purpose

How can we go about becoming happy at work? I know of many leaders who enjoy great success and are simultaneously very happy. All share certain common traits: passion, talent, and an inner desire to change things for the better. It is this personal "why" that lifts them up after setbacks. Like a magnet, it pulls them consistently in one direction and steers their actions accordingly. This personal why also serves as a compass: a trusted tool for decision-making. Having a personal sense of purpose—a why—is the surest way to a contented and happy life. "He who has a why to live for can bear with almost any how," wrote philosopher Friedrich Nietzsche in his own guide to purpose, *Twilight of the Idols*.

Though books like Simon Sinek's bestseller *Start with Why* have brought the idea to the forefront of popular culture, people have been asking themselves the question for hundreds of years (Sinek 2014). In Japan, the term *ikigai*—which loosely translates as "your reason for being"—has been used to refer to this search since the fourteenth century. In contemporary terms, we might express it as the reason we get up in the morning.

Exercise: *Ikigai*

Ikigai involves addressing these four central questions:

- What do you love?
- What are you good at?
- What can you get paid for?
- What does the world need?

As you reflect on these questions, try to recall some episodes in your life that you found particularly significant and impactful. What are the recurring feelings or themes in these stories? What stands out most to you? Ask your closest family and friends how they would answer the questions for you, too.

The intersection of your four answers is your ikigai, your personal reason for being. It will help you understand what drives you, so be sure to record your findings.

You will likely be unable to crystallize your why on the first try. This is normal. Your why is not some kind of precious find to be discovered and then conveniently stored away. Ikigai is a process; thus, it's important to give your why time to reveal itself to your conscious mind. As the weeks go by, you'll likely pick up new clues to work through in light of the existing ones. Michelangelo—who believed that every lump of stone exists with a work of art already inside it—was a master of this approach. For him as the sculptor, he believed the task of his eyes and hands was merely to uncover the hidden beauty. In the same way, you can uncover your why piece by piece. It takes patience, but this is to be expected: finding out who you truly are is no insignificant task. Do you want to bring people together? Revolutionize the world of work? Help others on their life and career paths? Protect the planet? Take the time to find your why.

Once you have found your why, you can get to work translating it into a concrete vision.

Making Your Purpose Tangible: The Impact of a Powerful Vision

A personal vision gives expression to our wishes, dreams, and unique purpose by translating them into vivid images. It provides direction and orientation. A vision is neither a collection of goals nor a strategy: it is a tangible picture of an ideal future. It might be a metaphor, a short story, or an immersive mental simulation of a day in our life in five or ten years' time. What are we doing on that day? What do we see? What do we feel? What do our family, friends, or colleagues have to say about us?

A vision should be tangible and should touch us emotionally. We might conjure up the feeling of giving the opening speech for the (still far-off) green tech division. We might feel the cold winter air of Davos as we attend the World Economic Forum in five years' time, presenting the results of a research project on artificial intelligence. We might see a classroom of hopeful young faces in Africa, the first cohort at a technical training center that—despite all challenges—is being worked on with high priority and will hopefully be open soon. While some of these visions project far into the future, they are expressly *not* fantasies. In fact, at one time, they were the concrete visions of friends, colleagues, and clients of mine, all of whom managed to make them a reality.

Sometimes we can have a vision without having the terminology to label it as such. Years ago, as a drummer in an indie rock band, I pictured that we would be wildly successful: I could feel our first physical record in my hands. I had what in today's terms would be labeled as a vision. As it happens, the hoped-for fame didn't transpire; otherwise, I would be producing an album in a California recording studio instead of sitting here writing a book. Still, we won a rock band contest in 1989 and released a live album along with other bands. I still have the record in my office today. It's proof that back then, my big vision—or at least its little brother—really did become reality.

Don't Be Shy; or, How to Formulate a Powerful Vision

An interesting requirement of formulating a vision is that we must perceive ourselves through the lens of our future potential. In this respect, it's important not to allow ourselves to be hindered by self-limiting beliefs. Writing on this subject, psychologist Carol Dweck contrasts the notion of a static self-image with that of a dynamic one—or, as she calls it, a "growth mindset" (Dweck 2017). To avoid limiting our opportunities for self-development, we must disengage from a static mindset—the idea that our talents and abilities are fixed and unchangeable. Imagine, for example, that your vision involves you undertaking public speaking, but you're aware that public speaking has not been your forte thus far. Don't let this limit your dreams. After all, it's perfectly possible not only to train your oratory skills, but to improve them beyond anything that might currently seem possible.

A dynamic self-image is a useful tool for continued development, since it entails openness to the fact that one day we'll be able to do the things we currently cannot. Cultivating a dynamic self-image means thinking beyond the limits of our current abilities and fostering positive beliefs that will help us along the way. If we see ourselves as unfinished—as *non finito*, as it's called in art—the scope of possibilities is almost unlimited.

Exercise: Formulating a Personal Vision

Write down how you see yourself in ten years' time, using the following questions to help you paint a picture:

- What have you achieved?
- What do others appreciate about you?
- What are you doing for work? What motivates you in your professional life?
- What values do you project to the world?
- Which principles do you live by?

Refer back to this vision from time to time and make additions and changes as necessary. If you undertake this exercise in earnest, you'll be surprised, at some point, at how many of your ideas have actually materialized. I can promise this from personal experience.

Making It Happen: Using a Vision to Effect Personal Change

Personal development and change do not occur in a linear fashion. Instead, they take place in distinct cycles that correspond roughly to the pattern of the Deming or Plan-Do-Check-Act (PDCA) cycle (see https://en.wikipedia.org /wiki/PDCA). The PDCA cycle describes a four-phase process for learning and improvement that can easily be transferred to the pursuit of personal growth. In each cycle, we compare our ideal self with our current self, then derive the new skills or habits we want to acquire or improve. After that, it is a matter of practicing, experimenting, and gaining experience. Eventually, the cycle begins anew.

Personal growth cycle

Growth Mode: The Parasympathetic Nervous System Is Activated

The starting point for each cycle is always our ideal self. This includes our dreams, values, and hopes as well as our purpose, vision, and the identity we aspire to have. These things function like guiding stars that provide us with energy and motivation. Not only that, but picturing our ideal self also triggers a neurobiological boost. When we engage with our dreams and the things we deem important, we activate the areas of the brain in which positive experiences are stored. The parasympathetic nervous system—responsible for building energy reserves and regulating recovery processes in the body—comes alive. The parasympathetic nervous system is associated with feelings such as joy, gratitude, and curiosity. It helps us to be optimistic, open to the new, and mindful of our strengths. This sets a positive mood for change and helps us cultivate the energy we need to grow beyond our current selves.

In Survival Mode: The Sympathetic Nervous System Takes Over

Unfortunately, many of us often proceed in a way that's precisely contrary to what was just described. This unhelpful response is intensified when, for example, we have taken on a challenging new role and are demanding too much of ourselves. We saw this with Jonas in our case study. In such situations, we engage exclusively with our worries and problems and trap ourselves in a negative state of mind. As a result, we activate the brain areas that store negative experiences. The sympathetic nervous system—responsible for regulation in stressful situations and for triggering the fight-or-flight response—swings into action. The sympathetic nervous system is associated with negative feelings such as fear and anxiety and, as a result, encourages pessimism and a tendency to focus on our weaknesses. When the sympathetic nervous system is activated, we switch into survival mode. This is not beneficial for personal development. Survival mode is incompatible with growing beyond ourselves.

Lasting change almost always begins with positive questions: those that deal with opportunities, dreams, hopes, and our personal vision. Studies by Richard Boyatzis, professor of psychology and cognitive science at Case Western Reserve University in the US, back this up. In his book *Helping People Change*, Boyatzis shows how effective personal change is enabled by starting with positive questions (Boyatzis, Smith, and Van Oosten 2019).

A personal vision helps us to consciously return to this positive state as often as we need to. As research shows, we can reinforce a positive mood by acting mindfully, spending time with good friends, laughing, going for a walk, and doing many other things. Even a pet can help. Getting into a positive frame of mind unlocks the door to personal change.

Vital Behavior Change: How to Succeed at Personal Transformation

Comparing our vision to our current reality provides clues about the skills we need to develop. If we want to become a rainmaker, like Jonas in our case study, we need to learn how to sell. If we want to be perceived as empathic leaders, we need to take time for our employees and learn to listen. If we want to transform an organization, we must be able to bring others on board with our plans. Embedding new skills requires regular practice—which is easier said than done, because even the best intentions quickly fall by the wayside amidst the distractions of day-to-day business. This is something I know from experience. The trick here is to change our behavior in such a way that we start to do the desired action automatically. To do this, we need to build new habits.

The Vision Starts the Engine; Habits Keep It Running

Almost half of the actions we perform each day are based on habits, not on conscious decisions. Habits are behaviors that we repeat automatically. Since we don't need to think about them per se, they relieve some of the burden from our brain and make everyday life a little easier. Habits form when we do the same actions repeatedly and, eventually, the decisions behind them become automated. When a process becomes habitual, this frees up time and capacity in the brain for other things. Journalist and nonfiction author Charles Duhigg describes this phenomenon very effectively in his book *The Power of Habit* (Duhigg 2013). Habits help to keep our "engine" running.

What follows are four rules of thumb for adopting new habits. These rules encapsulate all the wisdom I've learned in my endeavors to adopt new habits over the years. While I don't claim the rules are exhaustive, I can assure you they work very well in practice.

Habit Rule No. 1: Start with Your Strengths

In any attempt to change our behavior, there's a great temptation to start with our weaknesses. This, we believe, will be the quickest way to close the gap we've identified between our aspirations and current reality. Unfortunately, this notion is misguided. The changes we seek aren't about short-term improvements in performance but about holistic personality development, for which there are no shortcuts. As much as we might want to, we cannot reinvent ourselves overnight. For one thing, this change would be largely superficial, and we would fail to sustain it for long. For another, it wouldn't be credible to those around us.

Take the example of a CEO at a medium-size mechanical engineering company. A naturally somewhat aloof character, he heard that he was perceived as unapproachable at work and sought to resolve the problem immediately. He memorized the names of several of the workshop staff and greeted them by name on his next tour of the workshop. Back at his office, he received a call from the angry head of the union: some of the workshop staff had contacted the union with their concerns. To them, the fact that the normally tight-lipped CEO suddenly knew their names could mean only that they were about to be dismissed.

For effective personal growth, we must begin with our strengths, not our weaknesses.

When we focus on what we can do well—the things that come most naturally to us by virtue of our personality—we find change much easier to accomplish. In this example, it might simply have been listening that would have helped the CEO. If he had asked just one of the workshop staff questions with genuine interest and listened to them the way he listened to his fellow board members, he might have had a very different impact. The worker would have felt valued and the story would have rapidly spread, only this time with the positive effects he had intended.

Habit Rule No. 2: Concentrate on a Few Select Habits

It's a good idea not to take on too much at once. The best results are achieved by focusing on the small number of new habits that will bring the most change. This demands smart prioritization. For example, we shouldn't resolve to visit a customer more often in order to expand our network of contacts and, at the same time, to be more present at our own office and speak personally with employees to optimize internal visibility. Realistically, we can't accomplish these two things at once. By taking on too much, we run the risk of spreading ourselves too thin. Our batteries quickly become depleted and the implementation of our vision once again relegated to a distant prospect. The rule here is: less is more. In my experience, it is advisable to focus on no more than two or three new habits at a time.

Habit Rule No. 3: Continuously Work on Yourself

In much the same way that a marathon runner develops a training plan, many of my clients develop a personal program of learning. A learning program is a list of the habits we want to acquire in line with our vision. These should be small things that are easy to implement. It might be simple listening, as just described. It might be regular one-on-one meetings with members of our own team. It might be regular customer visits. Whatever it is, remember that success is not achieved overnight: it takes patience, persistence, and self-discipline. It can help to frame our efforts as a "continuous improvement process," with ourselves as the subject. If you've ever worked in a manufacturing company, you'll almost certainly know what I mean.

As a management consultant, I spent many years helping to improve my clients' processes. Sometimes it was about quality; sometimes about time or costs. Over time, I learned that it's not always the large measures that bring about the biggest impact. In many cases, the combination of several smaller measures is what unlocks the door to lasting improvement. *Kaizen*, which originated in Japan, is probably the best-known continuous improvement concept (see https://en.wikipedia.org/wiki/Kaizen). Literally translated as "change for the better," it's the philosophy of achieving perfection through consistent small steps. By contrast, rapid improvement based on one-time innovation sits on the other side of the spectrum. It's easy to see why the kaizen concept is much more relevant to the personal development domain. Instead of trying to change radically from one day to the next, it's far more realistic for us to aim to improve a little every day. This is how new habits are formed: bit by bit.

Habit Rule No. 4: Experiment with Cues

Unfortunately, the brain doesn't distinguish between good and bad habits. We cannot stop bad habits overnight any more than we can adopt new ones. However, we *can* act smartly based on the knowledge that every habitual action begins with a cue and ends with a reward. We can experiment with this cycle to get the results we want.

For one thing, we can make it harder for ourselves to access the cue, or trigger, for our bad habits. If, for example, we lose precious time every day to a flood of emails and have a bad habit of checking messages as soon as they land in our inbox, we might choose to filter our inbox using folders. Then, the emails we're cc'd on can be automatically redirected to a separate folder labeled "Can wait." If we don't see these emails in front of us, we won't be tempted to read them. Voilà—the cue is eliminated.

New habits can also be coupled to existing ones. If we usually start the day with a cup of coffee and a look at the newspaper, it might make sense to follow this up by calling one or two important customers. In this way, we create a chain reaction of good habits (Clear 2020). Another tactic is to reduce the hurdles and energy required to access new habits in the first place. If we want to make a habit of reading technical articles on a new subject, we might consider placing the articles within easy physical reach. This will make the desired habit more accessible.

Insofar as our habits are visible to others, they also become part of our reputation. This logically means that by changing the former, we can also change the latter. In one example, a client of mine had taken on a new role as CEO of a medium-size company. He was considered experienced, intelligent, and an excellent speaker, but at the same time rather reserved.

This, of course, made it difficult for him to establish the close relationships he needed with the company's uppermost two levels of management. He decided to make a small adjustment to an existing routine. Instead of going directly to his office in the morning, as he had done in the past, he chose a longer route through the building that took him past the offices of the executive team. With each executive he encountered, he spent a couple of minutes engaged in conversation. He gradually came to be perceived as "actually, a very approachable person after all." By changing his habits in a small way, he made a positive impact on his reputation in the company.

Exercise: Establishing New Habits

Call your vision to the forefront of your mind once more, then consider the following questions:

- What two or three new habits (no more!) would help you move toward your vision?
- To which existing habits could these be coupled?

Begin acting on your findings over the next seventy-two hours.

Vibration: How to Sustain the Energy for Change

A few years ago, a friend of mine wanted to learn to play the piano. He saw himself sitting with his family around him, performing a beautiful Chopin piece. There was no doubt that this was a wonderful vision. After finding the right online piano tutor, he set to work, brimming with motivation and willpower. From then on, he resolved firmly, he would make a habit of practicing for at least two hours three times a week. Come Christmas at the latest, he thought, he would be able to perform his first piece. For the first week, all went according to plan. By the second week, two practice days had been canceled due to urgent client appointments. The third week he wasn't able to practice at all—and so it went on. At some point, he gave up in frustration. Does this sound like a familiar pattern?

When Willpower Alone Is Not Enough

Unfortunately, good intentions and willpower are not enough to effect lasting positive change. Those who attempt change with these tools alone tend to underestimate their own inertia and overestimate their willpower. We exert large amounts of willpower in order to begin a new habit at all. Later, like a muscle, willpower becomes fatigued when it continues to be exerted over time. In mechanical terms, we can liken this to the transition from static friction—when two objects are at rest—to sliding friction, when two objects are in motion. Sliding friction is less than static friction at rest, but it still costs energy. The acquisition of new habits follows a similar pattern. Even once we have motivated ourselves to set things in motion, we still remain far from our goal, because there is always resistance to be overcome. For this reason, we need a system that maintains the momentum for change and provides timely nudges. Behavioral economics, which combines psychology and economics, can help.

"Nudges": How We Can Outsmart Ourselves

In his bestseller *Thinking, Fast and Slow*, Nobel Prize winner Daniel Kahneman describes the two modes of thought that influence our decisions (Kahneman 2011). We are dominated by the fast thinking of System 1, which works in an automatic manner based on associations. System 2 is slower and works in a rational, reflective way. We require both modes of thinking to master the complexity of life.

The problem is that System 1 is able to ambush System 2 and to construct a story that System 2 finds credible. We refer to this as *cognitive* or *narrative bias*. Such bias leads us, for example, to overestimate ourselves, to see the past through rose-tinted glasses, or to attribute accidental successes to our own competence. This is a toxic blow for the resolution to acquire new habits. We might say, "Ah, it's not so bad if I skip the new market reports this week," despite the fact that we had resolved to read them every week from then on. To ensure that we continue with a new habit, we need an effective push at the critical moment.

One of the key principles of behavioral economics—including when changing the behavior of entire groups—is what's known as a *nudge*: a prompt for the new behavior. Authors Richard Thaler and Cass Sunstein brought this subject to popular attention with their aptly titled book *Nudge* (Thaler and Sunstein 2017).

Nudges must be designed and activated such that they prompt us toward the desired behavior at the critical time. To create a nudge, we must first simplify a new habit as much as possible and break it down into small, concrete steps.

Imagine, for example, that the desired habit of keeping in touch with customers becomes the concrete plan to meet customers for lunch three times a week. This action must then be linked to a nudge. In this case, the nudge might be calendar entries that are managed by a secretary and serve as a dependable reminder. Some people also ask a friend or colleague to provide a regular nudge.

It's better to use nudges to initiate desirable behaviors than to punish negative ones. Consider, for example, the case of a plant manager known for his casual approach. His resolution was to stop interrupting his employees when they were talking. To motivate him, he put a piggy bank on the desk in front of him and placed a euro inside it every time he failed. He intended to use the proceeds to buy cakes for his department. A noble idea, maybe, but it didn't work out: in fact, it had quite the opposite effect. After a while, the plant manager took pleasure in patronizingly depositing €10 notes. He began deliberately interrupting his employees rather than merely doing it reflexively. His negative behavior was further reinforced by the misguided nudge.

Today, there are a variety of digital nudges available in the form of apps for establishing new habits. Known as *habit trackers*, these apps typically offer a combination of automatic reminders and user-friendly dashboards for tracking progress. Some of the most popular include Habitify, Strides, Coach.me, and HabitHub. For many years, I personally found success through a small slip of paper in my wallet combined with an Excel spreadsheet with simple metrics. The piece of paper, which reminded me of the new habits I wanted to form, found its way into my hands every time I opened my wallet to pay for something. Colleagues occasionally asked what was on this mysterious slip of paper. Whenever someone asked, I told them—and I automatically gained another person to keep me accountable going forward. I used the Excel spreadsheet to track my progress and rewarded myself when I reached interim goals.

A regular nudge increases our chances of persisting with a new habit. However, rhythm is the tool with which a new behavior is properly anchored.

Rhythm: The Key to Effecting Seemingly Unthinkable Change

On Tuesday, April 12, 1831, the 60th Rifle Regiment of the British Army completed a maneuver and returned to the barracks for lunch. In neat lines of four, seventy-four British soldiers made their way across the Broughton Suspension Bridge near Manchester, whistling happily and marching in step. The bridge seemed to resonate with their rhythm, encouraging the soldiers to march more briskly still. Then, disaster struck: the structure collapsed and forty of the soldiers fell into the River Irwell. Twenty were injured, six of them seriously. The excessive vibrations triggered by the marching rhythm had caused the bridge to give way. To prevent similar disasters in Germany, it's still forbidden, under Section 27 (6) of the Road Traffic Regulations, to march in step on bridges today.

> In physics, a simple rhythm can unleash unimaginable amounts of force—enough to bring down several-ton structures. By the same principle, rhythm is the key to effecting seemingly unthinkable personal change.

Rhythm is a central and ubiquitous element of our lives. The seasons run according to a rhythm, as do day and night and the cycles of high and low tide. In his book *Sync*, physicist Steven Strogatz presents extraordinary examples from physics, biology, chemistry, and neuroscience that illustrate the steady beat and synchronicity that bring order to the chaos of the universe (Strogatz 2003). Thousands of fireflies gather along the tidal rivers of Malaysia and blink in unison. The rotation of the moon on its axis is perfectly aligned with its orbit of the Earth. Our hearts beat thanks to the synchronous firing of tens of thousands of pacemaker cells. Rhythm plays a role everywhere. If we want to recharge our batteries for personal change, we must take advantage of this powerful phenomenon.

Research also shows that the forming of new habits is significantly more successful when a rhythm is created and consistently maintained. Put another way, it's better to take a small step every day than a big step once a week. "Do something, not everything," as a coach once told me. As a rule of thumb, we shouldn't skip a new habit more than once in a row in order to avoid breaking the rhythm. If momentum is destroyed before a habit is established, we're not likely to maintain it for long. Consistency is the key to success.

By taking small steps and pursuing small goals, we create a series of small but significant successes.

Every time we perceive that we have succeeded, we're motivated to continue and the learning effect is reinforced. We feel that things are going to plan, and gradually the new habit becomes established. Psychologists Seppo Iso-Ahola and Charles Dotson characterize this concept as "psychological momentum" (Iso-Ahola and Dotson 1986). Their studies show that previous success in sports competitions not only enhances performance and self-confidence, but also increases the chance of emerging as the winner. Small steps also have a rather simple advantage: it's harder for us to find excuses to avoid taking them.

Given the importance of momentum, it's not surprising that documenting and visualizing our progress also reinforces our chances of success. Perceived progress brings satisfaction, joy, and happiness as well as increasing our self-worth and encouraging us to view the world in a positive way. For all these reasons, it is a powerful motivator. Harvard professor Teresa Amabile, the author of extensive research on the subject, refers to this as the "progress principle" (Amabile and Kramer 2011). It underpins the inclusion of extensive dashboards on habit tracker apps, where users can easily view progress on a daily, weekly, or monthly level. When the user is made aware of their progress, they are fortified with energy for the road ahead: they resonate with themselves, so to speak. The combination of small successes, breakthroughs, perceived forward movement, and the achievement of goals makes the whole system vibrate in sync, generating forces of change that are far greater than the sum of their parts. Little by little, the new habit sinks deeper and deeper into the subconscious.

Becoming a Master at New Habits

When we experiment with a behavior that we want to make a habit, it's likely to require effort at first. This isn't surprising, because we're moving beyond our comfort zone. According to the twenty-one-day rule, which is based on findings by plastic surgeon Maxwell Maltz, we must commit to a new behavior for twenty-one consecutive days in order for it to take root in our psyche. Moreover, it's important that we don't simply go through the motions of a new behavior arbitrarily. To improve, we must practice it mindfully and with purpose. This is the way to become a master.

Our brain is adaptable and plastic, like a muscle. As with muscle training, we get better when we practice things outside our comfort zone, at the limits of our existing abilities. It's then that the learning effect is particularly powerful and we experience a motivational boost. In response to this, the brain creates new neural connections; in layman's terms, its structure is changed. This means we have the power to mold the brain in exactly the way we want to and thus to achieve perfection in our chosen tasks. In their book *Peak*, authors Anders Ericsson and Robert Pool show that everyone is capable of acquiring new skills at an outstanding level through deliberate learning (Ericsson and Pool 2017).

The more complex a new habit is, the longer it can take to develop. With this in mind, we must be patient and maintain the initial rhythm, even when we face repeated setbacks and frustrations. At the start of a new habit, in particular, it is important to regularly check in and take stock of our current state. If we seize every opportunity to work on a new habit, remain steadfast in the face of setbacks, and consciously engage with repeated cycles of trying, failing, and learning, we will eventually acquire exactly the skills we need.

In a nutshell:

- A vision gives expression to your wishes and dreams by translating them into vivid images. It makes your personal why tangible.
- If you want to change, start with positive questions that deal with your hopes, opportunities, and dreams.
- Habits help you acquire the skills you need to turn your vision into reality.
- You acquire new habits by continuously working on yourself, focusing on your strengths, and experimenting with useful cues.
- Willpower alone is not enough to bring about and sustain positive change. Over time, willpower becomes fatigued, just like a muscle.
- A nudge can help remind you to persist with a new habit at a critical moment.
- The power of rhythm and visualization can be used to bring about changes you might never have thought possible.

For the Curious among You: Where Jonas Is Now

Jonas has expanded ChemCo into a major customer account: the first big consulting project was followed by several more. He has also built a close relationship with ChemCo's board, including the CEO. As for his internal status, Jonas is considered one of his firm's most successful partners of recent years. This has hugely increased his self-belief. He's still working on his reputation as a rainmaker, and the joint presentation with the ChemCo CEO remains a vision for now. He is, however, well on his way to realizing it.

Rigorously Test: Experimenting with New Identities

It's not every day that you buy a new car. A test drive is vital to ensure that the car you buy is the one you're actually looking for.

–MOTORING ASSOCIATION ADAC, 2021

At one time or another, you'll likely think about getting a new car. Perhaps the problems with your old car have been multiplying; maybe you want to switch to an electric model. Before you make your purchase, you'll almost certainly take one or more test drives. Test-driving is an important concept in professional development, too.

As leaders, we need to be prepared to reinvent ourselves as required by the times. The reluctance to do so in a timely fashion is our fifth career stopper. As with taking a test drive to overcome our uncertainty about a potential new car, we should try out new jobs in advance. We might learn something surprising—just like Yvonne.

Case Study: Yvonne

It's a sunny day at the beginning of June, and Yvonne and I are meeting for our third coaching session. In-person meetings are permitted once more, so our session is taking place at my office.

"So, how was the homework?" I begin.

"Actually, I have a surprise to tell you about," Yvonne replies. Then, mysteriously: "And a crazy idea. It's something I've been dying to discuss."

Yvonne has proven exceptionally successful as a marketing manager for MediaCo, a telecommunications company, where she is part of the talent pool in the internal development program. But while she enjoys fantastic career prospects, she's not happy in her role. She feels constrained by the rigid corporate structures; her gut feeling tells her that something is wrong. She has been thinking about a career change for some time, but isn't sure exactly where to go. The aim of today's session is to narrow down some options for her change of professional direction. In preparation for this session, Yvonne has begun to think about alternative jobs.

The Background—and a Crazy Idea
I offer her a coffee: Yvonne is a self-proclaimed "coffee junkie."

"Go on, then," I say. "I'm excited to hear it."

"Okay. The surprise first," Yvonne laughs, "since I really can't keep it to myself any longer. Last week, a recruiter called me. He wanted to talk to me about becoming the European head of marketing for a French media group. It would be quite the career jump. I would lead a larger team than I do today and would be responsible for the marketing of several divisions. I have to let them know by tomorrow if I'm interested and want to continue the talks."

"Congratulations. Honestly, with your qualifications, I'm not surprised. And what do you feel instinctively? Do you think it's right for you?"

Yvonne hesitates for a moment, then replies with a thoughtful expression. "I know what I'm about to say sounds terribly stupid, but to be honest, I'm not sure."

"Why stupid?" I ask.

"Because I know I won't get another chance like that in a hurry. I told a friend about it. We know each other from college, and she works in marketing too. She said I'd be crazy not to take the opportunity."

"And why do you think it might not be right?"

"It's only a gut feeling; I can't pin it down." Yvonne shakes her head. "It would be a big corporation again, and that's not what I'm looking for."

"I can understand that," I say. "So, let's leave it for a moment. Tell me about your crazy idea."

Yvonne looks a little embarrassed, then suddenly begins to smile. "I hardly dare say it," she begins, "but I'd love to become an entrepreneur. To be honest, when I think about it, I'd love to start tomorrow." Her gaze clouds over again. "But that's probably even more stupid. I'm not an entrepreneur, my business ideas probably won't work anyway, and it doesn't make sense with my current path."

"Who says it doesn't make sense?" I ask.

"Well, I've invested a lot of time and energy in marketing. All the doors are open to me there. Wouldn't it be madness to give it up overnight and start my own company—especially now, when I have the chance of making a jump like that?"

"But something's telling you that the entrepreneur route might be an option, right?" I counter. "Otherwise, you wouldn't be entertaining it at all."

"You're right. Part of me is looking for adventure, and another part of me is holding myself back. I really struggle with that feeling sometimes. I feel torn."

"Could it be that your own story is holding you back?" I ask.

Yvonne looks a little puzzled. "What do you mean?"

A Change of Direction as a Positive Differentiator

"There's a story about Yvonne in which she's building a career in marketing and moving up the ladder," I say. "You know this story; it's the one you're clinging to right now. It's also the story told by people who know you, which perhaps makes you cling to it even more. But what if there were another story about Yvonne: an Yvonne who, at some point, decides to pursue a career as an entrepreneur. Exciting stories are built on unexpected twists and turns. If you look at the biographies of successful female entrepreneurs, you'll see there are elements of their professional lives that only make sense together in retrospect. What might appear in the moment to be a radical change of direction becomes part of a coherent whole when you look back."

Yvonne seems thoughtful. For a moment, she is completely silent. Then, in a quiet voice: "This plan would take a lot of courage, and I don't know if I have that. How do I even know if I'm fit to be an entrepreneur?"

"Do you remember your character strengths from the 'Values in Action' test we talked about last time?"

"Yes," says Yvonne. "Well, I can remember three of them: leadership, creativity, and drive."

"Exactly. Research says that leadership and drive, for example, are among the typical character strengths of successful entrepreneurs. You have a classic entrepreneurial profile, I can assure you. You might not even know what you're made of yet."

"And how can I find out?"

"By experimenting, perhaps."

Yvonne looks at me in complete astonishment. "Experimenting?"

Experience through Experiments

"Yes, experimenting," I say. "If you want to know whether you're an entrepreneur, you'll have to try it out–like test-driving a car. Thinking alone won't get you anywhere. And if you find that you're *not* an entrepreneur in the process, you can always continue your marketing career."

"And what kind of experimenting might I do?" Yvonne asks.

"Anything that will give you clues about yourself in that role," I reply. "And of course, what you can accommodate timewise alongside your current job."

"I think I've got an idea already." She is enthusiastic. "MediaCo is sponsoring a female founder event: I could get involved in that. I've been asked to participate anyway."

"That sounds perfect," I encourage her.

"There's something else, too. There's an online entrepreneurship course I've been wanting to take part in. The list of participants was really exciting. Another course is going to start soon, this time with live meetings as well."

When the ideas start flowing, they don't stop. When searching for experiments, it seems, Yvonne is entirely in her element. We create a long list of ideas, then set about prioritizing.

"It seems like you have an interesting journey ahead of you," I say.

Yvonne is smiling. "I'm excited!"

"And what are you going to say to the recruiter? Do you want to talk to them again?"

"I'm going to cancel," she replies. "In fact, I've just made the decision now. This is my first experiment: I'm making this decision as a future entrepreneur."

"Are you sure?" I press.

"I couldn't be more certain," comes the decisive reply.

"Fantastic!"

She laughs, then adds: "And if it all goes wrong–well, I'm blaming you. Our conversation today made me think my crazy idea might just be possible!"

Ready for the New

In the months that follow, Yvonne leads a double life, so to speak. Alongside her role as marketing manager, she takes an entrepreneurship course at a leading business school, attends start-up fairs, gets involved in the Female Founder network, meets an old friend who works at a venture capital firm, and gets to know faces from the entrepreneurial world. In our coaching sessions, we reflect on her experiences and the options her experiments have opened up. Almost ten months later, after a break, we meet again for a further session.

"I've got another surprise," she begins.

I smile. "I wouldn't have expected anything less. Go on, I'm dying to know."

"I've decided to quit!" From the look on her face, I can tell this decision is a happy one.

"Your own company?"

"Not quite," says Yvonne, "but close. I'm going to join a green tech start-up. It's a crazy story, to be honest. I met an investor at an entrepreneurship event, and she put me in touch with the two founders. Both of them are experienced and well connected. When I got to know the team, there was an immediate spark. My gut feeling was a resounding 'yes!' They've just finished a financing round, and they're looking to professionalize the company. I'm going to be part of the management team, and I'll have overall responsibility for marketing and strategy. It's like the role was made for me." She is bubbling with excitement as she shares her news.

"Congratulations!" I say. "It sounds fantastic. Remember, I told you a job would come along just when you were ready for it."

"Now I know what you mean," she says, beaming.

"In the absence of champagne," I suggest, "shall we toast to it with a coffee?"

Yvonne looks a little shy. "Do you have green tea instead?"

"Of course. Not a coffee junkie anymore?"

"An experiment," Yvonne says, laughing.

What We Can Learn from Yvonne

▶ *We gain experience in a new thing from experimenting, not from simply mulling it over.*

Yvonne found herself in a dilemma. On the one hand, she had a fantastic chance to continue building her career in marketing; on the other, she felt a niggling desire to break away. She made a wise choice to listen to her gut feeling and reject the offer from the French firm: it would have been more of the same, and she wouldn't have been happy there. At the same time, she was initially unsure about her entrepreneurial potential. Mulling over these doubts at length would have gotten her nowhere. Instead, she followed the far preferable approach of test-driving the possible career change with practical experiments in a protected space. Only by doing so did she build the necessary self-belief to make the change for real.

▶ *Change means taking a journey of exploration and meeting new people.*

Yvonne's environment was not conducive to her desire to reinvent herself. On the contrary: she had built a reputation as a marketing expert in the company and the industry. Her identity was fixed in this environment, her future path mapped out. The friend she asked for advice had this same fixed image: she was unable to imagine Yvonne outside of a marketing role. As a result, while Yvonne remained in this environment, she couldn't hope to receive the moral support she needed. It was keeping her chained her to her old identity. Before she could reinvent herself, she first had to expand her network to find people who could support her in this desire.

▶ *Those who want to reinvent themselves must question the narrative of their own success.*

Yvonne was trapped in her existing story and saw her path as if she were in a tunnel. For this particular story, there was only one "happy ending": arriving at the top of the marketing ranks. Yvonne was wary of any deviation from this path, since for her, that option was tinged with the likelihood of failure. This is why she didn't trust her inner voice at first. In order to recognize and move beyond this restrictive view of the world and, in doing so, to open herself up to a new professional identity, she needed external stimuli and new experiences. Only then did she realize that her story could continue successfully in a completely different way.

Keep reading to the end of the chapter to find out where Yvonne is now.

On Experimenting, Exploring, and Emerging Stories

A current Google search for "reinvent yourself" shows well over two million hits. It is little wonder: according to a study from the Organisation for Economic Co-operation and Development (OECD), around 14 percent of today's jobs will disappear in the next fifteen to twenty years due to automation. Another 32 percent will change radically as a result of digitalization (OECD 2019). In this context, the willingness to reinvent oneself and adopt evolving professional identities becomes an important factor for career success. But how can we go about doing this effectively?

Here, we can draw usefully on a scientific method developed over four hundred years ago by English philosopher Francis Bacon (Bacon 2017). This method involves making a hypothesis, testing it through experiments, evaluating the observations, and drawing conclusions. Following the same model, we can first experiment with new professional identities, then use the experience we gain to inform our decision about a new path. As part of this process, it's important to embrace a journey of exploration, meet new people, and be open to an unexpected retelling of our own story.

Experimenting: Act First, Think Later

In 2013, the then CEO of Deutsche Telekom AG, René Obermann, gave up his post and moved to a much smaller Dutch cable network operator in order to be "closer to the engine room" and return to an operational role. Many people dream of starting over and doing something different, even when they seem to have achieved everything they could want. I have met many of them. They are the board member who wants to try their hand at a start-up; the marketing manager who dreams of becoming an architect; the sales manager who has crime writing on the brain.

Many of these dreams come to nothing due to a fear of change or a lack of self-belief. We think too much. We spend too much time analyzing whether a new job will suit us, focusing on our weaknesses more than our strengths. We hesitate, feeling torn between a well-paid, stable position and the niggling urge to look for something new. In the end, we remain where we are—in a job whose expiration date may have long since passed—and end up doing nothing at all. This is why it's better to start with action over thought—even if, in practice, it can be an uncomfortable shock to the system at first. I learned this early in my career—and was fortunate to be able to do this learning in a protected space.

Acting into a New Way of Thinking

It was Monday, January 19, 1998, the first day of my MBA program in Paris. A marketing lecture was on the schedule that morning, and the expectant MBA class took their seats in the lecture hall. "This is no place to learn the basics of marketing," Professor Bardot proclaimed as he entered the room. "The place to do that is on the streets." He divided us into teams and assigned each team a topic for a local market analysis. We had twenty-four hours to gather information, evaluate it, and prepare a presentation—without any marketing knowledge at all. For me at least, it was a baptism by fire. After an intense day and a very short night's sleep, the teams gathered to present their results. It was incredible what everyone had managed to put together. Most importantly, we had learned more about marketing in those twenty-four hours than any lecture could have taught us. We had moved from acting to thinking and not, as is customary, in the opposite direction.

What applies when it comes to learning new disciplines is even more apt for learning about ourselves. To discover who we are and what we are made of, we must take concrete actions and try out new things. Theoretical musings are of limited utility; rather, the success or failure of reinvention depends on the experience we gain to inform our ideas. Herminia Ibarra, professor of organizational behavior at the London Business School, summarizes this concept neatly in her book *Working Identity*. She says we are much more likely to act ourselves into a new way of thinking than to think ourselves into a new way of acting (Ibarra 2002). This means that we have to experiment!

Design Thinking, Applied to the Self

In our experimentation, we can draw on the design thinking approach from agile product development and the *minimum viable product (MVP)* concept popularized by Silicon Valley entrepreneur and author Eric Ries in his Lean Startup methodology (Ries 2012). An MVP enables us to complete the feedback loop of build-measure-learn quickly and effectively. Unlike traditional product development, the MVP isn't about perfection, but about an accelerated learning process and the testing of business hypotheses. We can think of it as following the empiricist tradition established by Francis Bacon.

Framed in these somewhat unconventional terms, we can become the MVP in our own experiments. Our experimentation is not, after all, about validating an already perfect new version of ourselves, but about setting in motion an effective learning process. Reinvention is not a linear process that can be planned in advance from start to finish. Rather, our experiments should take us out of the realm where we feel stable and safe and require us to "surf the edge of chaos" (Pascale, Millemann, and Gioja 2000). This is the place where innovation and discovery occur.

> In order for something new to emerge, our experiments must succeed in moving us consciously out of our comfort zone.

Each time we pass through a learning loop, we gain important new information that we can evaluate in order to build our conclusions. To do this, we can ask targeted questions, such as:

- What have I learned?
- Which of my hypotheses have been confirmed? Which have not?
- Did I feel energized by the new experience?
- How did the people around me react?
- What new ideas emerged?
- What would I do differently next time?

Each new cycle allows us to test a different version of ourselves and to draw corresponding conclusions from the answers. As is customary in design thinking, we should begin by placing all options on the table and doing as many experiments as we can. We must discover and explore before narrowing things down.

"Reinvention Lite": Old Job, New Identity

We don't always have to change jobs to reinvent ourselves. We can also find a new professional identity by redefining an existing job—as the following example shows.

A Client's Tale of Reinvention

There came a time when a client of mine, an experienced managing director of a medium-size company in the automation sector, began to feel increasingly constrained by the monotonous nature of his day-to-day work. One cost-cutting program followed the next; the company seemed solely preoccupied with internal matters and was losing market share. He found it increasingly difficult to create momentum and motivate himself. He decided to take the radical step of redefining his role as managing director, namely by establishing himself as a bridge builder to external partners. Instead of filling his schedule with internal meetings, he spent the following months talking to young start-up entrepreneurs, meeting millennials for lunch, and traveling to Silicon Valley. In his vision, he saw a new strategic direction for the company and a new identity for himself as a modern leader. To achieve it, he had to conduct the right experiments and open himself up to new ideas and a new style of leadership. By radically questioning his old approach and personally embodying the change he wanted to see, he transformed his company into a genuine high-tech player in the space of just a few years. At a personal level, he gained a whole new beginning.

Good Surprises

As we experiment, we may uncover dormant skills and abilities we would never have imagined we had. There can be various reasons that this is the case. Perhaps we've not yet had the opportunity to use them, or maybe we've obscured them so much that we're unable to access them in the course of normal day-to-day life. Developmental psychology describes the development of dormant skills—driving a car, riding a bike, playing golf, or virtually any other activity—in terms of the four stages of competence. As beginners, we start at the level of *unconscious incompetence*: we don't know what we don't know. In the second stage, *conscious incompetence*, we *do* know what we don't know: things click into place, the proverbial penny drops, and we begin to learn. From there comes the third stage, *conscious competence*: we know what we know and are able to apply it; we practice it consciously. By the last stage, *unconscious competence*, we've internalized what we've learned and do it naturally without being aware of it. The behavior change is embedded and will persist (see https://en.wikipedia.org/wiki/Four_stages_of_competence).

If our experiments reveal that there are certain skills we perform unconsciously, it might be worth returning to the previous learning level in order to become fully cognizant of what we know. These skills could be surprisingly valuable. One of my clients discovered his ability to attract and develop talent—a gift that research shows characterizes the most successful leaders (Collins 2001)—through his involvement in a mentoring network. This gift helped him make the next jump up the career ladder.

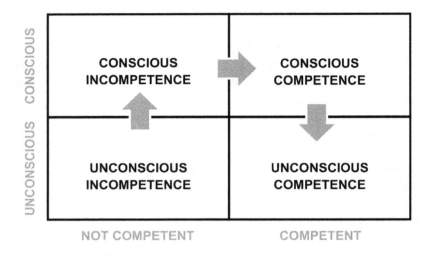

<table>
<tr><td></td><td>NOT COMPETENT</td><td>COMPETENT</td></tr>
</table>

The four stages of competence

Making a Job a Platform for Change

The desire to reinvent ourselves doesn't materialize from nowhere. Often, an external stimulus inspires us and triggers a desire for change. This stimulus could be collaboration with people from other disciplines, involvement in a project outside our usual field of expertise, participation in a conference, a visit to a university or business school, a TED Talk, or a book. By making our job a platform for experiments and looking beyond the horizons of familiar terrain, we open ourselves up to new discoveries. We see our role in a much more innovative light.

Advanced Reinvention: New Identity, New Job

Imagine that you are highly successful and have achieved more than you ever thought possible. You are currently in discussions regarding several new roles. You receive a great deal of appreciation for your work. Things couldn't be going better—apart from the unexpected feeling that something isn't quite right. You try in vain to ignore it, telling yourself that you should be more than satisfied. You reproach yourself for being ungrateful for all that you've achieved. Yet this vague discomfort not only persists, but gets stronger. Your job begins to sap more of your energy. Slowly, the problem starts to crystallize: you no longer feel any connection to your job at all. You have all the external recognition you could hope for, yet the fire has gone out and cannot be rekindled. What to do then?

Embark on the search for a new professional identity.

Some of my coaching clients, friends, and former colleagues have experienced this phenomenon. In many cases, the process began several years before they actually left the job. This is not unusual, as research shows. On average, three years elapse between the decision to leave a company and the final day of work. The interim phase can feel like "living inside a hurricane," as Herminia Ibarra puts it (Ibarra 2002). The problem we face during this time is that we know the professional identity we want to discard, but aren't exactly sure how to find a new one.

Of course, the obvious thing to do in such situations is to cut corners and call a recruiter or to look at job ads online. This approach tends to be unsuccessful, because it forces opposing interests to meet head-on. While the candidate is looking for a new identity, the recruiter is interested only in the old one; after all, this is the one that they can sell. At best, we end up with "old wine in new skins": doing the same job at another company and pondering why, after a few years, the fire is still out. To reinvent ourselves, we need unconventional means and, above all, time. In practical terms, here's what this means.

The search for a new identity must begin before we quit an existing job.

There are a few caveats here. First, we must be extremely well organized if we wish to experiment successfully with a new professional identity alongside our regular work. Second, there's the question of personal energy.

On the one hand, if we opt to reinvent ourselves in an existing job, we can expect advantageous synergy effects. Experimentation with a new management style, for example, will take place largely in the course of our day-to-day work and may well bring about positive results. By contrast, if we're seeking an entirely new professional identity, these synergy effects don't apply. In this case, we must not only expend energy on our current job, but reserve additional energy for experimentation in the new space.

In my experience, there are three possible routes we can pursue when experimenting with professional identities alongside an existing job: a temporary sideline activity, part-time training, or a sabbatical.

Temporary Sideline Activity

A temporary sideline activity gives us the chance to engage with new topics or projects alongside our day-to-day work and, through this, to experiment with new identities. Take the example of a client who, in addition to his role as head of quality, set up an internal resilience training program for managers in his company and later established a successful business in the field. For my own part, I was involved for many years in recruiting and career development alongside my consulting work, which is how I discovered my passion for career management. The advantage of a sideline activity is that it delays the need for radical steps until we're sure. Thus, the experiments take place in a largely risk-free environment.

Part-Time Training

A variant on the preceding option is to study or train alongside work. This route provides structure and entails regular exposure to a new subject that may, in time, become a new vocation. In one example, a former client of mine—then a manufacturing manager—studied business psychology alongside his day job and later set up a business as an organizational consultant. In another example, a former colleague trained as a photographer alongside his consulting work and realized his dream of owning his own photo studio.

The Sabbatical

If we require more time, more energy, and—crucially—more distance from our current role than it is possible to obtain while working, a sabbatical can be an advisable option. A sabbatical affords us the necessary breathing room to think about the future. In one case, a former consulting colleague used a sabbatical to experiment with the idea of founding a private equity company with friends. The sabbatical gave him the opportunity to engage in depth with the various facets of an investor's role and to test the strength of his interest in the markets. After the experiment concluded with positive results, he ventured directly into self-employment. Today he is one of the leading midcap investors in Germany.

How a Former Colleague Found His Vocation

While many of us need time to ascertain the direction of a radical change, there are other cases where a new identity—a genuine calling—radiates clearly for all to see. A former colleague in our New York office was one such example. He was a talented consultant, but his real passion was music. He eventually succeeded in making it his profession. His name is John Roger Stephens, but you likely know him better by his stage name: John Legend. He is one of the few artists who has won an Emmy, a Grammy, an Oscar, and a Tony award, the rare quartet of achievements known as an EGOT. Many years after his career change, once he was famous, John performed a special concert for us in the quasi-familial setting of a partner meeting. He talked about his unusual path from consultant to music star. For me, he's a wonderful example of how a person can find and pursue their true identity and calling.

Exercise: Experimenting with Unconventional Topics

- Go to a bookstore and buy a book on a subject you wouldn't normally read about.
- In the upcoming quarter, give a presentation on a topic for which you're not a subject matter expert. Deliberately place yourself out of your comfort zone.
- In the next three weeks, commit to a project that's not in your area of expertise.
- Once you've completed the exercises, write down what you learned. Which of your learnings will you take with you?

Exploring: Why Colleagues Won't Help Us with a Change of Job

When looking for a new professional identity, we need people who will support us emotionally and with sound advice. We need people who inspire us and will help us in our search to recognize and develop ourselves. We need people who, like us, may be questioning their path. By acting as catalysts, these people can have an important influence on the outcome of our search. The bad news is that they likely can't be found in the world we currently inhabit. We need to make new connections and contacts and to venture to the edges of our current network.

An Experiment: Ten Days without an Identity

A few years ago, I participated in a ten-day silent retreat. It was not only the meditation that made it an illuminating experience. It is highly unusual to spend ten days in a confined space with one hundred others, sitting next to each other for many hours a day without exchanging a word. You know what these people look like, how they sit on their cushions, what they eat, and how they move, but not their names, nationalities, languages, ages, or professions. You can build a vague picture of them based on visual clues, but you can't categorize them neatly in the way that we as humans are so inclined to do. After ten days, when the silence is broken and you have the chance to learn who they are, you quickly realize the extent to which a person's profession defines how we perceive them. I understood firsthand how readily we tend to pigeonhole others, even those we don't know much else about.

Forget About Friends and Colleagues

A person's professional identity helps us to slot them neatly into our preexisting view of the world and to form an initial opinion. This process is inevitably influenced by the bias of stereotypes. "Oh, so you're one of those," I was often told when I introduced myself as a management consultant.

Our profession is a kind of figurehead. It shapes our social identity and how we are perceived in social groups, such as colleagues, friends, and family.

Members of a group derive their own social identities—and thus their own self-image—partly from their fellow group members. For example, some of your friends likely not only value you as a person, but also are proud to have a doctor, banker, or board member in their inner circle. In some traditional social clubs, your professional identity becomes your official ticket into the social group. Your family, too, perceives you not just as a wife, husband, mother, or father, but as a lawyer, engineer, financial controller, or whatever else you might do. It's what your children tell others about you at school.

When we begin redefining our professional identity, this has the inadvertent and indirect effect of tinkering with the fabric of social groups and calling into question other members' images of themselves. It's little wonder, therefore, that we encounter skepticism and hostility. If an individual decides to quit their job as a board member of an IT consulting firm in order to pursue a spiritual path, they typically can't expect to rely too heavily on the enthusiasm and broad support of friends and colleagues. Family, for their part, may be the most resistant of all. While many people will be unable to comprehend the rationale behind the step, family members may have additional concerns related to the individual's ability to earn a living. Moral support must therefore be sought elsewhere. (This example, by the way, is the true story of a former meditation teacher of mine who quit their job as an IT executive to found a meditation center.)

The people around us may try to talk us out of taking the step toward a new professional identity. "Don't do it!" a fellow engineer said many years ago, when I told him of my plan to leave my position as head of a business unit and start again in a consulting firm. "It's a mistake; you'll regret it for the rest of your life." It was well-intentioned advice, but it was misguided, because I haven't regretted my decision even once.

It's also possible that colleagues and acquaintances will lose interest and allow contact to lapse in response to a change in our professional identity. They were proud to know the partner of a renowned accounting firm, for example, but the new founder seeking investment for a start-up doesn't quite carry the same social cachet. These human disappointments cannot be avoided, especially in the case of more radical career shifts. This is something I have personally experienced. While there can certainly also be positive surprises—welcome gestures of support from sources we wouldn't have expected—remaking a professional identity almost always entails seeking inspiration, moral support, and practical advice outside our usual circles. To do that, we need to make new connections and contacts.

The Revolution Begins at the Periphery

When seeking inspiration for a new professional identity and initiating the process of personal change, we must venture to the bounds of our existing networks and talk to many new and different people. As we know from history, the Reformation didn't begin in Rome: Luther posted his Ninety-Five Theses on the Castle Church of Wittenberg, a place hardly anyone in the Catholic capital would have heard of at the time. Radical change often begins on the periphery, not at the center. The same applies for personal change.

Motivation for transforming our professional identity is often found in places where we don't normally look or listen—in exchanges with designers, artists, entrepreneurs, programmers, or perhaps even political activists. "Hang out with freaks!" said management guru Tom Peters (Peters 2002). By spending time with visionaries, thought leaders, and pioneers on the edges or entirely outside of our usual networks, we allow ourselves to draw a line to the future, gain inspiration, and broaden our horizons. This can provide the initial impetus for personal change.

Exercise: Expanding Your Network

- Over the next three weeks, have lunch with three people you wouldn't normally meet: an artist, a start-up founder, or a competitor, for example.
- Join a new virtual group on, say, LinkedIn or Twitter. Listen to talks and participate in the subsequent discussions.

- Reestablish lost contact with friends, particularly those who have pursued completely different paths than you.
- Resolve to get to know at least three new people the next time you're invited to an event or party.
- Reflect on the conversations you had as you worked your way through these exercises. What new ideas did you take away? Which will you pursue further?

Be open to every new contact you encounter and experiment widely with your network. As entrepreneur and Virgin founder Richard Branson said, "The person with the skill set you need to get your new business idea off the ground may be sitting at the next table in the café. Go over and say hello" (Branson 2014).

Role Models, Navigators, and Moral Support

Once we have gathered our initial ideas about a new professional identity, there are three types of contacts who can help us experiment further: role models, navigators, and moral supporters.

Role Models

Role models provide the inspiration for professional identities we may not have considered before. They are motivating figures who not only speak about their profession with enthusiasm, but serve as a credible example. On my path from engineer to consultant, for example, I was inspired by a management consultant who had previously been an engineer himself and had pursued this radical transition in a manner I found most persuasive. It was he, too, who gave me the idea of undertaking an MBA program.

Navigators

Navigators point us in the right direction by helping us to connect with new people. To do this, they need a broad and dense network. Unlike a role model, a navigator's own professional identity is irrelevant: what matters is that when we speak to them about a possible career change, they not only show interest and understanding, but propose the names of several other contacts who can help us. On my path to becoming a coach, I was supported by a number of navigators: people who connected me with experienced coaches with similar résumés to mine. The inspiring conversations that ensued gave me the impetus to train as a coach myself. Today, I pay forward this support by using my own personal network to help executives seeking a change.

Moral Supporters

The final piece of the puzzle is to obtain moral support for our project. As you've seen, it may not be realistic to expect this support from those immediately around us. Instead, perhaps the best moral support comes from peer groups: like-minded individuals who find themselves on comparable paths and likely have similar dreams and goals. My own experience indicates that the opportunity to exchange ideas and experiences is a fantastic motivator and means of confirming one's plans. Attending my coaching training in London, for example, I was surprised I was able to meet so many executives from different industries who had been thinking about the same things as me. We had embarked on our search at similar points in our careers, asked similar questions, and read some of the same books. This invaluable peer exchange motivated me to continue along my new path. Moreover, it laid the foundations for the very strong network from which I still benefit today—from the discussion of new ideas to matters of business development.

How a Colleague and I Grew Our Network Overnight

Sometimes a world of contacts can open up in an instant if only we're willing to take the first step. A few years ago, I collaborated with a colleague on a professional article about the trend for meditation among executives. It was written essentially on a whim, but was picked up by various industry magazines around the world and generated a tidal wave of response (Greiser and Martini 2018). We had been wholly unaware that our interest in the subject was shared so widely. New contacts materialized overnight. There were invitations to conferences, conversations with companies and executives far beyond our existing networks, and connections to cross-industry working groups and political institutions. These inspiring exchanges led to a new in-house mindfulness training program—and of course, to the next article. It was an avalanche effect whereby each contact we generated opened up its own world of opportunity. My colleague, encouraged by the success, later decided on a new path as a coach and meditation trainer.

When we cultivate the development of new contacts, these contacts often propagate to form whole new networks over time. We meet ever more people who represent what we ourselves would like to become. Through these exchanges, our own thinking begins to change—and just as when we experiment, we move from and via action into new patterns of thought. Almost unconsciously, we begin to gradually adopt the new professional identity.

Emerging Stories: How We Can Give New Meaning to Our Narrative

During my time as a recruitment director in consulting, I read countless CVs of graduates and experienced lateral movers. What particularly interested me were the unexpected twists and turns in the course of a life: an economist who had founded a diving school in Asia, a physicist who had initially studied theology, a banker who had once been a professional athlete. Many of them later became very successful. Such departures from an established career path are not uncommon, including among the world's best-known leaders. US businesswoman Sheryl Sandberg began as chief of staff at the US Treasury Department before moving to Google and Facebook and later becoming a best-selling author. Similarly, Bill Gates's resume shows an unexpected transition from Microsoft founder to philanthropist. Both were able to reinvent themselves and retell their own stories in unexpected ways.

Those who seek to reinvent themselves must not allow themselves to be stifled by the constraints of their existing story. Who says that a journalist must always be a journalist, a lawyer always a lawyer, an engineer always an engineer? We must be open to retelling our story based on the findings of our experiments and, through doing this, to imbuing it with new meaning.

Successfully reinventing ourselves, however, has one vital requirement: we must break away from conventional notions of success and career. Here, once again, we encounter a paradox.

The Authenticity Paradox

As leaders, we must, above all, be authentic. We encounter this mantra again and again in leadership literature and at business schools. In the context of personal change, however, it is less clear how authenticity should be judged. As we pursue change, are we moving outside our comfort zone and learning—or are we behaving in an inauthentic way and pretending to be something we're not?

If we want to reinvent ourselves, we can't be limited by who we are today. Whether we seek to redefine ourselves in an existing role or to pursue a completely new professional identity, we must transcend our current self-image and the constraints of the story we have mapped out in our head. Initially, at least, this process necessarily entails seeing ourselves as an unfinished product and thus moving out of our comfort zone. The problem is that the more we move out of our comfort zone, the more our familiarity-seeking inner voice will attempt to pull us back. *What's the point of you being here?* it might say. *Stop pretending; keep being who you really are.* Research shows, however, that learning often begins with what feels at the time like unnatural and superficial behaviors. Paradoxically, in order to grow as leaders, we must do things that an absolutist approach to authenticity would reject (Ibarra 2015). Only in this way can we achieve the goal of developing a future version of our authentic self.

> In practice, we can develop a future version of our authentic self by being open to learning from others, acting in the here and now, and testing different versions of our own story.

Learning from Others

"Good artists borrow, great artists steal," the painter Pablo Picasso is reported to have said. This applies to leaders, too. While we don't wish simply to become a poor imitation of another leader, neither should we hold on to a supposed "true self" that prevents us from moving forward. Rather, it's important to observe role models and examples closely in our own experiments, and to adapt, refine, and recombine individual elements until they fit. Eventually, we'll attain a new version of our authentic self that is credible to us and others.

Acting in the Here and Now

By acting entirely in the here and now, we become authentic. By contrast, if we think too much before we act, the thinking leaves an indelible trace. The activity is marked from the outset by a preconceived idea and a certain notion of right and wrong, of authentic and inauthentic. As Zen teaches us, we can avoid these shadows by doing something completely. Like a good bonfire, we must burn ourselves completely so as not to leave a trace of ourselves in what we do (Suzuki 1999).

Testing Different Versions of Our Own Story

The first requirement of an exciting story is that we don't know what the ending will be. Exciting stories are built on unexpected twists and surprises. As a rule, a good story follows the four-part sequence of situation, disaster, turning point, and happy ending (Etzold 2020). Later events give meaning to the preceding events in retrospect. The same principle applies to our life story. A professional failure does not necessarily herald the end of a career, but can instead mark a turning point in the overall narrative. The biographies of entrepreneurs like Arianna Huffington and Steve Jobs are prominent examples of this. By testing different versions of our own story, we can imbue our previous actions with new meaning. When we look back, these actions reveal themselves to have been authentic and meaningful after all.

In my experience, how we engage with our own story plays the biggest role in any attempt to reinvent ourselves. If we can retell this story credibly and give it new meaning, we are taking a major step toward becoming the new version of our authentic self.

Breaking Free: Liberating Ourselves from the Constraints of Our Story

The narrative of our life explains who we are, who we are becoming, and the path we're taking to get there. It gives meaning to our lives. We can change this narrative; it isn't fixed. To do this, however, we must free ourselves from stereotypes and self-limiting notions of career. Drawing inspiration from the economic principle of *creative destruction* devised by Joseph Schumpeter (https://en.wikipedia.org/wiki/Creative_destruction), we can change an outdated narrative of ourselves by reinterpreting elements of our life path to date and connecting them in new ways. By considering parts of our story in light of what we now know, we can reframe it to be consistent with the future we see for ourselves. Seemingly incongruent actions gain meaning. In this way, we solve one of the central identity challenges of a career change: that of combining the old and new identities. This is illustrated by the following example.

Career changes are common among those working in management consultancies. Barely a week goes by where I don't receive a farewell email from a colleague. Many see their time in consulting as a springboard for a career in industry or a private equity firm, or for starting their own company. There are surprising changes, too—like Philip, a former colleague of mine from BCG's London office. At the height of his success, while walking on the beach, Philip suddenly had doubts about whether he had truly found his calling. After a period of intense reflection on a possible new path—with all the attendant emotional ups and downs—he decided to give up his prestigious job as a partner and offer his talents and skills to a completely different institution: the Church of England. Philip gave new meaning to his story and continued to write it in a way he hadn't previously foreseen. I recommend listening to Philip's talk, "Finding Your Personal Mission in Life," at https://youtu.be/g93NhV33Mhw.

> We cannot change our life story from one day to the next. In most cases, a gradual approach is required in order for the existing story to flow meaningfully into the new narrative.

It might be significant experiences—positive or negative—that herald important turning points. It might be that we recognize the turning points only in retrospect. We might need to take a step back in order to move forward again. We might require an array of seemingly random experiments and tests until we finally achieve clarity on where our story is supposed to go. Whatever path we take, following it consistently is the key to revealing a new version of our authentic self. When we do, we can rightly say that we have reinvented ourselves.

Exercise: Tell Your Own Life Story

Imagine you are approaching a roundabout. Each exit corresponds to a possible route for your professional journey:

- Exit 1: Realization of a childhood dream
- Exit 2: A surprising career turn
- Exit 3: Turning an unconventional idea into reality
- Exit 4: An exciting but risky path

Think about the options that each path represents. What opportunities and possibilities would be open to you in each? What other exits might exist farther down each road?

Now cross out the exits that are categorically not an option for you. Imagine your future story in the context of each remaining option and how it might represent a meaningful trajectory in light of your path so far. Write these stories down and return to them for occasional reflection.

In a nutshell:

- If you want to reinvent yourself, you must begin by experimenting with new professional identities—just as if you were in a lab.
- Start by acting, not by thinking. You discover who you are, your innermost self, primarily by doing.
- To reveal new information, you must experiment outside your comfort zone.
- You can test out a new identity in an existing job by radically questioning yourself and experimenting within the bounds of your environment.
- If you want to experiment in an existing job, consider a sideline activity, part-time training, or a sabbatical.
- Your established network and closest contacts will likely be unhelpful in your search for a new professional identity. Move to the periphery.
- You can rewrite your professional story by reinterpreting the meaning of your path so far.
- If you want to rewrite your own professional story, you must break away from strictly conventional notions of success, career, and authenticity.

For the Curious among You: How Yvonne Is Doing Now

Yvonne has found exactly what she was looking for: a highly dynamic entrepreneurial environment, an inspiring team, a corporate culture characterized by openness and personal responsibility, and a very broad scope of responsibility. In her own words, she has learned more in her first year at the start-up than in her last three years at the corporate group. In the meantime, the start-up has grown considerably, and calls from recruiters have multiplied since her move. She regularly receives interesting offers. The new story she has to tell makes her even more attractive to the market.

Restart: Accelerating Out of a Break

If you take your vehicle out of service and keep it parked for a period of time, be aware that some parts might not work as expected once you get the car back on the road.

—WEB.DE GUIDE TO CARS & MOBILITY, 2016

If your car spends a long period out of service—perhaps because you've taken it off the road for the winter, or you now work from home and no longer commute to work—problems may arise when you try to get it going again. The battery may be dead and you may have to push the car. When returning to work after a long break or embarking upon a new life phase, you can face similar challenges. It is naivete in tackling such problems that represents our sixth career stopper. Failing to prepare properly risks a false start. Wolfgang's story shows just that.

Case Study: Wolfgang

"I hope you can coach outdoors, too," Wolfgang says, laughing. "I always get my best ideas in the fresh air. Here, I've reserved a nice quiet spot for us. Good to see you."

"Welcome back," I say.

It's a sunny day in July, and Wolfgang and I are meeting for our second coaching session. At his request, we are meeting in a very pleasant beer garden. We sit undisturbed at a table to the side. More than two months have passed since our first conversation. In the interim, Wolfgang has fulfilled a lifelong dream of hiking across the Alps from Munich to Venice.

The Background

Just under a year and a half ago, at the age of almost sixty, Wolfgang made the decision to resign from the CEO role in a family business. He had repositioned the company in the years prior and almost doubled sales. Having done that, he felt it was time to hand the reins to the next generation. At the time, he had scarcely begun to ponder what he wanted from the third phase of his life: he had simply looked forward to a time without deadlines and had hoped to let the rest come naturally. That hadn't quite worked out as expected. Wolfgang now has a supervisory board role and a visiting professorship at a university, but feels that this isn't enough. He still has a lot of energy and is looking for something that truly fulfills him. The goal of our coaching is to provide clarity and impetus for this next phase of his life.

Restarting His Engine

Of course, before we get down to business, we spend some time discussing his hike. "Do you still want to look for something new?" I ask, "or did the hike change your mind?"

"I'm sure," says Wolfgang. "I want to get the engine going again."

"Have you thought about potential options?"

"To be honest, for the first three weeks, I didn't think about any of that," Wolfgang says. "I just wanted to enjoy the mountains with my backpack and my hiking boots. But when I was walking through the vineyards in Veneto, approaching Venice, the subject suddenly reentered my mind. I remembered an Italian colleague from years gone by; we used to share our dreams for retirement. He wanted to become a winegrower. I don't know what became of that. When I got to that point of my hike, I had a few thoughts about what I might do myself, but I didn't really get very far."

"Might winegrowing appeal to you, too?" I ask jokingly.

Wolfgang laughs. "I like wine a lot, but becoming a winegrower . . . My passion doesn't quite go that far."

"What would you enjoy doing in this third phase, then?" I ask.

"Well, for one thing, I'd like to use my experience to make a positive contribution. After a year and a half, I'd hope I wouldn't be completely out of practice yet. I still know how to build businesses, how to run them, the challenges you have to deal with. But I don't want to go back to the corporate world; if I were going to do that, I could have just extended my contract. A seat on the supervisory board is enough for me. I'd rather do something else, give something back."

As Wolfgang speaks, I jot down a few keywords on a beer mat: *building businesses, leadership, giving back.*

"Are you making notes for your own retirement?" Wolfgang asks. I see the characteristic humorous twinkle in his eye.

"You know the old joke," I reply. "Consultants ask to borrow your watch to tell you the time." We laugh, then I continue: "Don't worry, all rights are reserved to you. I'm just taking notes; we'll need them in a minute."

"I'm curious to know what we're going to do," Wolfgang says.

The waiter brings two glasses of beer and two pretzels. We each take a first sip.

"What else would you enjoy, then?" I ask him.

"My daughter works in a start-up in Berlin—quite a different world from the one I know. We disagree quite often on business. I come from a world where it's all about sales and costs. For her, it's about *evaluation*, as she says. Still, I think I've been able to help her with a few tips on occasion, and I find her job fascinating. I'd love to get involved in that type of thing, though I think I'm probably far too old."

I note *start-up* and *help* on the mat.

"And what else?" I probe.

"Hiking!" says Wolfgang, laughing. "Seriously, I've loved the mountains since I was young. They're an important part of my life. But that's probably not relevant to this conversation."

"Who knows?" I say. I write *hiking* and *mountains* on the coaster. Then: "Can you think of anything else?"

"You want me to be specific, don't you?" he says. "I know for sure that it should be something meaningful. Other than that, I can't think of anything for now."

I write down a final keyword: *meaning.*

The Plan on the Beer Mat

"Great," I say. I push the beer mat over to him. "Let's go again from the top. Tell me again what you want to do, but this time without using any of the words I've written down."

Wolfgang looks at me wide-eyed. "Is this another one of your weird and wonderful coaching tricks?" He scans the list of words on the coaster: *building businesses, leadership, giving back, start-up, help, hiking, mountains, meaning.* Then: "Okay, I'll give it a shot. I still know a thing or two about making money. I like bringing people together to create and grow something new. I find it fulfilling to nurture young talent, and I love nature." Wolfgang looks as proud as if he had just solved the Riddle of the Sphinx. "I didn't do badly at all, did I?"

Again, I write. *Making money, creating new things, nurturing, nature.* I push the beer mat back to him. "And if you were to sum all this up in one word," I ask, "what would that word be?"

"You're really testing me now!" Wolfgang says. He thinks for a moment, then suddenly his expression brightens. "Growth," he says, "it all has to do with growth. I've always been driven by the challenge of growing a business. I enjoy watching people grow, and I love watching nature grow. I think, actually, that it's growth I've been missing in this last year and a half of retirement."

"It sounds like that would be a perfect metaphor for your fresh start," I suggest. "Growth."

"That sums it up very succinctly," comes the enthusiastic reply. "The problem is how we make it happen."

"What are your ideas, then?" I ask.

Wolfgang and I devise a long list of possible ideas for incorporating growth back into his life: sitting on the advisory board for a start-up, becoming an angel investor, expanding his visiting professorship at the university, or setting up a mentoring network for founders. We also develop more unusual ideas, like organizing mountain tours for young executives.

"Instinctively," he says, "I like the ideas of investing in the environmental sector and setting up a mentoring network the best. Perhaps I could even combine them. That would really get the engine running again." He laughs. "I've got the feeling my retirement might be even more 'active' from now on."

The Engine Restarts: From Beer Garden to Bold Action

In the months that follow, Wolfgang develops his ideas. He reestablishes old contacts and talks to investors, venture capital firms, professors, and associations. He researches initiatives and attends events for angel investors. Wolfgang learns a lot of new things. In December, we meet again for a further coaching session.

"I'll be thinking back to our coaster session in the summer for a long time," he begins. "Growth was the keyword I needed all along. I feel like I've got my engine running again; the hiatus is over. There's a concrete idea in place—and I've found two comrades in arms."

"I'm very excited to hear it," I say.

"I'm going to be working with a former recruitment consultant and a former colleague," Wolfgang explains. "We're going to build a platform that brings together start-ups with capital and expertise. Of course, we're not the first people to do this, but we can offer access to top-class mentors through our network. We're also going to focus on investments in the ecological sector: that's where my love for nature comes in. And all three of us have the same burning desire to start again with something new. You could have covered a few coasters if they'd been here with us!" He smiles. "So even in my old age, I'm fulfilling my dream of becoming a founder."

"That sounds fantastic," I reply. "You see, that's how it can go some-times, from walking to working on growth . . ."

". . . with Wolfgang!" he interjects, laughing out loud. "That's what I'll call my memoirs, then."

What We Can Learn from Wolfgang

▶ *Those who want to be active in retirement should reignite their engine for success at the right time.*

Wolfgang had to tackle the challenging transition that is part of every career: the step from respected top manager to retiree. The fact that he took this step voluntarily, to make room for the next generation, speaks to his great-ness as a leader. However, it was naïve to assume that a fulfilling activity for retirement would simply drop into his lap. Wolfgang would have been well advised to prepare for this major step in advance, because it brings with it considerable repercussions. These include negative psychological effects triggered by the sudden loss of power and influence as well as a shift in the values around which one's life is built. Wolfgang sensed this in his desire to be "needed again" and to be able to give something back.

▶ *Achieving momentum after a long break requires significant driving force.*

Wolfgang had been "off the road" for a year and a half. While he managed to swing back into action fairly seamlessly, an easy transition can't be assumed as a matter of course. Wolfgang had the advantage that his professional net-work was still in place and that he possessed the necessary driving force for the restart. Both literally and figuratively, his hike had afforded him distance and prevented him from losing himself in rumination. This had certainly been a risk. In addition, he used the energy and motivation that a long-distance hike brings to get started with his plans immediately afterward. In this way, he managed to beat the customary inertia after a long break. Books such as *I'm Off Then* (Kerkeling 2006) by Hape Kerkeling or *Über die Berge zu mir selbst* (*The Journey Across the Mountains to Myself*) (Wötzel 2009) by Rudolf Wötzel, a former investment banker, describe experiences similar to the one Wolfgang had.

▶ *Those who seek a restart after "turning the corner" into retirement can benefit from a metaphor that encapsulates what they're trying to achieve.*
To find fulfillment, Wolfgang first had to understand what was important to him in the third phase of his life. Once he did so, he needed a succinct way to encapsulate these ideas. Our beer mat exercise helped him reveal his personal metaphor: growth. Prior to this, it had been obscured under a web of ostensibly unrelated goals, likes, and passions. His metaphor provided a sense of orientation and triggered a surge of driving force. It made clear where he was, where he wanted to go, and how he could get there. After that, Wolfgang was completely in his element again. He succeeded, somewhat belatedly, in bringing about a new start for the third phase of his life.

Keep reading to the end of the chapter to find out where Wolfgang is now.

On (Re-)Activating the Engine for Success, Achieving Momentum, and the Act of Turning the Corner

Periods in which the pause button is pressed and success enters a standstill can occur in a number of forms. A sabbatical, for example, is a good way to recharge our batteries or devote time to taking care of family. Depending on the duration of such a break, we may first need to restart the engine before continuing to pursue our goals afterward. This process must be distinguished from that required after involuntary interruptions, such as being laid off. Here, too, a restart is required, but achieving it requires a different focus: getting out of the inevitable mental slump. Finally, there is the time-out from success that occurs after turning the corner into retirement. If we can accomplish a new start in our third phase of life, as Wolfgang did, this time-out doesn't have to be final.

(Re-)Activating the Engine for Success: How to Power Up after Time off the Road

Ten days of silent meditation in the Blue Mountains, a beautiful family trip through Australia and to the Great Barrier Reef, twelve books read, and (finally) more time to play golf and meet friends: this is how I spent my three-month sabbatical during my time as a management consultant. This time-out was an integral part of my time as a partner and afforded me the chance to recharge my batteries. It was one of the highlights of my professional life.

In many companies, such career breaks are no longer all that rare. Studies show that these breaks are used primarily for mental and physical rejuvenation, personal development, and traveling, but also for caring for relatives or looking after children (Statista 2017). The duration varies from a few weeks to several years. Time off creates distance from one's job and, depending on how we spend it, can help us to refocus and recharge our batteries. So far, so good—if only the return to the office didn't come afterward. For me, this felt like a hard landing after weeks in paradise.

Back in the office, I first had to fire up the cylinders again. In practical terms, this meant working through an overflowing inbox, returning the calls of numerous clients, holding dozens of internal meetings, and getting new consulting projects off the ground. I had been absent for almost three months, after which it took me almost twice as long to get things running again. Moreover, I was fortunate to be able to return to the same position and pick up where I left off. This isn't always the case. Returning after a break can be much more difficult than it was for me.

Four Weeks or Five Years? The Vast Spectrum of the Career Break

There are many different types of career breaks, each with different attendant challenges for the return to work. All have one thing in common.

The longer the break, the more difficult it is to continue seamlessly afterward—and thus, the more planning is required.

Sabbaticals: Opportunities and Stumbling Blocks

My own career break was taken as a sabbatical. There are various forms of sabbatical: unpaid leave, special leave, salary sacrifice, part-time work, and working time accounts (Allrecht 2019). A sabbatical may last for varying periods—from a few weeks to a year—depending on the form. Provided that an employee is willing to suspend their contract of employment and manage their own health insurance, pension contributions, and Social Security contributions, a sabbatical could theoretically be realized for an indefinite period.

The more we prepare in advance of the return, the easier it will be. As a rule of thumb, returning to work after a sabbatical of up to six months—perhaps even a year, if there's an appropriate agreement with the employer—should be relatively smooth. One friend of mine was able to reach an agreement with his employer for a one-year sabbatical during which he fulfilled a long-held dream of sailing around the world. A former colleague took a year off and built a children's home in South America. Both resumed their careers without issue afterward.

In cases where a sabbatical of several years is desired, the contract of employment can be suspended. The alternative, of course, is to give notice and later look for a new job. Both options are potentially problematic for the further course of one's career, since not every future employer will show understanding for an extended career break. For this reason, I recommend considering in advance whether and how you can convincingly explain such a "resume gap." We must avoid it becoming an insurmountable hurdle at all costs. There's another point to consider when taking a longer sabbatical, too.

The world does not stop turning in our absence.

In returning to the working world, we don't want to evoke shades of Austin Powers—the charming time traveler from the past in the James Bond spoof of the same name—whose catchy sayings and sixties worldview didn't quite fit with the present. Where a career break lasts for several years, this danger is undeniably real—not least because the "half-life" of skills has never been as short as it is today. Digitalization and artificial intelligence are changing the working world at a breathtaking pace; just consider, for example, the global spread of videoconferencing apps such as Zoom and MS Teams, which occurred at an unprecedented pace. By removing ourselves from this world for six months or longer, we risk losing touch and finding it difficult to catch up. To compound this, the market environment is changing ever faster. Valuable, hard-won expertise on customers, suppliers, and competitors can become obsolete after as little as a year.

There is another, even more obvious disadvantage of long breaks: they cause us to get out of practice. If we haven't driven for five years and want to get back on the roads, it's sensible to practice with the supervision of an experienced driver. Workplace skills can become similarly rusty.

Fortunately, there are warning signs that can alert us if a break is becoming too long. As a client of mine put it: "I suddenly found that the recruiters stopped calling. That's when I knew it was time to roll up the beach towel and get back to the office." Sabbaticals are like medicine: in small doses, they have a healing and career-enhancing effect. In excessive doses, they can be harmful.

Taking a Break between Jobs

Often, the period between leaving an old job and starting a new one can provide a good opportunity for a short sabbatical. This time off usually has to be negotiated with the new employer, bearing in mind that this employer likely has a high interest in a rapid start. If, for example, the new corporate strategy is to be finalized as soon as possible and your input was required yesterday, a request to spend six months traveling around the world likely won't be met with understanding. Perhaps, on this occasion, you'll have to make do with an in-state vacation. Even if the break is brief, though, it's advisable to take advantage of one between jobs: such an opportunity may not come around quickly again. To ensure smooth career progression, consider keeping the break to a maximum of approximately one month (Zucker 2021).

Sometimes, of course, this break is unexpectedly longer. A friend of mine, then an investment banker, resigned from his employer to join a competitor and was immediately put on "garden leave"—that is, a mandatory leave of absence for the period of his notice. This meant three months at home and a lot of free time. In some industries—where the current employer needs to cut off access to sensitive business data and customers—this is quite common. In my friend's case, he used this break to finally spend more time with his family.

Start Planning Parental Leave Early

Parental leave is another form of career break. In terms of later career progression, it's one of the trickiest types of all to manage. Even today, career and family are difficult to reconcile—and it's often women who give up a career or experience a professional downturn after the birth of a child. Studies show that statistically, the chance of women with children finding their first management position ten years after graduation is almost halved, while children are almost never associated with a career downturn for men (Klüver, 2016). This is also referred to as the "mother gap." Although the proportion of men who take parental leave is increasing significantly, it's doing so from a very low base level (Statistisches Bundesamt 2019).

While parental leave comes with special protection against dismissal, the return to work is still a major challenge. Many management positions are designed to be staffed full-time, making them unviable for parents who also want to take care of their children. Even a part-time position can be challenging, especially if the work is time-intensive and difficult to predict. Take the case of a friend of mine, who returned to her partner role in a professional services firm at 60 percent of full-time hours after her parental leave. While her employer readily facilitated this model, there was an unexpected hurdle to be overcome: she had to defend the model to clients in order to reduce her travel and protect her regular family time. As you might imagine, these clients weren't always receptive. In addition, at a personal level, she was mentally torn between children and career and found herself with a permanent guilty conscience. This period was among the most difficult of her entire career.

> **!** To ensure that a return to work goes smoothly and to minimize any career downturn, it is important to start planning as early as possible and to consider what you want to happen after the leave.

During periods of parental leave, it's advisable to keep in touch with colleagues, use the time for further training, and periodically make contact with your employer to convey your continued interest in the job. If manageable, working part-time during parental leave can be a useful way to keep your toe in the water. Above all, it's important to review your situation at regular intervals, to adjust to setbacks without knocks to your confidence, and to remind yourself of your proven knowledge and skills. Incidentally, the friend whose story I shared still works in professional services—and has since become one of the company's most successful partners.

"I'm Back!": Planning a Successful Return

What could be so difficult about returning? After all, there's such a thing as too much preparation. It's possible to overthink things; it's probably best just to let things happen. Others will be happy that I'm finally back, and things will run smoothly, just like before. . . . These may be tempting thoughts, but they're wrong!

Particularly after an extended period of leave, we can't simply march back into the office as if we had merely gone out for some fresh air. For one thing, the office will have changed. While the building and furniture may look the same, there will have been significant changes to colleagues, processes, organization, and technology. For another, we'll probably have changed as well. The distance afforded by a professional sabbatical gives us a new perspective, one that may also come with different expectations and values. Perhaps we now see things in a more nuanced and relaxed way; perhaps we're no longer prepared to make compromises that would have been tolerable in the past. We must prepare mentally for such changes, and this necessitates effective planning.

In my experience, returnees must typically grapple with the following questions:

- What are my personal goals? What are my expectations for the next professional chapter?
- What are my career options now, anyway?
- What do I need to relearn? What new skills do I need?

- Who can support me in my return?
- How much time will I have for family now?
- How can I make the transition as seamless as possible?

It's important to take sufficient time to address these questions. In the course of my work with clients, I've developed a tailored six-step structure for this purpose. It has proven effective in preparing for career reentry after an extended period of time away.

1. Reactivate your network.
2. Explore your options.
3. Take time to set realistic goals.
4. Update your skills.
5. Regain confidence with the right mindset.
6. Navigate the unknown and be ready to learn.

The acronym RETURN symbolizes the six segments of the wheel that will transport you back onto your professional path. Keep in mind every element of the acronym as you make your return journey.

Step 1: Reactivate Your Network

Of course, it won't be possible to maintain all of your contacts during a break; if you did, it wouldn't be a break at all. Before you return, though, you should reactivate your network of colleagues and customer contacts and talk to as many people as possible. This will help you start the new phase with momentum. If you're looking for a completely new job, reactivating your network will often lead to offers to discuss opportunities.

Step 2: Explore Your Options

Particularly if you can't or don't want to return to your old job, you must carefully evaluate your career options. What are you particularly good at? What do you enjoy doing? Where are the best opportunities? How and where could your professional story continue after your break?

Step 3: Take Time to Set Realistic Goals

Take some time to flesh out your personal goals and expectations for the next phase of your career. Do you want to continue on your previous path or pursue a new direction? What are the things you want to achieve in the future? How do you now define success and fulfillment? How do you want to divide your time between work, family, and leisure? The more specific you can be about your goals, the more successful your return to work will be.

Step 4: Update Your Skills

As they say, a rolling stone gathers no moss. Returning to work requires you to preemptively refresh some of your skills and competencies, since these will likely have grown a little rusty in the interim. There may be some newly developed gaps in your knowledge that need to be filled. To achieve this, it can be helpful to read as much as possible, take online courses, and perhaps attend some relevant events. As part of this step, you should also carry out essential admin tasks like bringing your documents up to date and refreshing your CV.

Step 5: Regain Confidence with the Right Mindset

Before you return, it is vital to honestly examine the extent to which you're mentally ready to step back into the fray. How have you changed in the meantime? Which of your values have shifted? Which of the old compromises are you willing to continue making, and which are you not? Where will you draw the red line in the future? What is the consequence if it is crossed? This step is all about returning with confidence, with a mindset that is conducive to success.

Step 6: Navigate the Unknown and Be Ready to Learn

Be prepared that there will still be lots to learn, since you won't be able to fill *all* the gaps beforehand. There will be unexpected surprises: new colleagues, new customer contacts, new organizational units, changed processes, new apps, and a new data security policy. The more willing you are to learn, the faster you'll feel at home in the new (old) world.

Exercise: Preparing to Return to Work

Using a rating scale from 1 to 6–where 1 is very good and 6 is insufficient–rate yourself honestly on how well you have prepared in each area. Next, connect the lines to form your wheel.

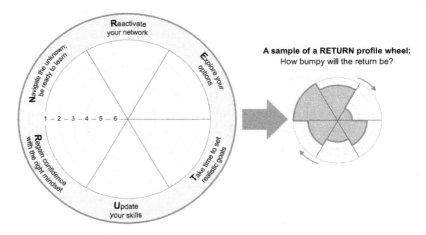

A sample of a RETURN profile wheel:
How bumpy will the return be?

The RETURN model

- Look at your wheel and imagine it as a tire on the car you're using to RETURN to work. How bumpy will the ride be?
- What is the diameter of your wheel? Are you returning on a scooter or in a car?
- Where is there still a need for improvement?

Achieving Momentum: How to Make a Fresh Start after a Career Setback

The news came as a complete surprise. A client of mine, the head of development at a mechanical engineering company, had just returned from vacation. He was reinvigorated and brimming with motivation. On his first day back, a board member asked for a meeting—and served him his walking papers. His position, as it turned out, had been eliminated as part of a restructuring program. The news came as a complete shock. It marked the beginning of an unexpectedly lengthy search for an equivalent management position in another firm.

An Unexpected Break

Sometimes the pause button is pressed involuntarily and unexpectedly. Losing a job is among the most traumatic experiences a person can undergo in their professional life. This applies even more for top managers, those who have devoted their lives entirely to their careers and suddenly find themselves completely adrift. Whether the dismissed party has played a role or the decision is entirely the result of unfortunate external circumstances, the attendant challenges are similar. It's always painful to go through a time when one's career curve ceases to move upward.

While I have been fortunate enough to avoid this particular fate, I have had plenty of opportunity to engage with the thorny matter of job loss up close. For one thing, I have supported clients through situations such as the one just described. For another, I witnessed many colleagues in consulting who were asked to leave. As noted earlier in the book, top management consultancies work according to the "grow or go" or "up or out" principle. If an employee doesn't meet the criteria to progress to the next level, they're automatically required to leave. During my many years in internal career development, I was jointly responsible not only for these decisions, but for breaking the bad news to the colleagues involved. From junior consultants right up to partner level, it was my job to inform them they had failed to progress and that their career with us was therefore over. These discussions were among the most unpleasant experiences of my professional career, but there was unfortunately no way to make them more palatable. When big dreams are shattered in an instant, this understandably triggers an emotional response. This holds true even if the decision has been in the offing for a long time.

> At the moment in which the dismissal becomes real, it's diffi-cult for the affected person to accept it. The disappointment and the embarrassment of rejection are too great.

In such situations, I found it helpful to convey appreciation and grati-tude to the colleague and to promise support in getting them back on their feet. Every employer, in my view, has an obligation to do this.

There are also cases in which the affected person feels a certain sense of relief from the dismissal. This is the case, for example, if it puts an end to a lengthy phase of uncertainty. It applies if the employee had repeatedly toyed with the idea of quitting but was ultimately unable to bring them-selves to do so. It also applies if an employee was already visibly on the sidelines and had ceased to feel like they were contributing at all, making every new working day a kind of torture. "You know, I'm glad the decision has been taken away from me," as a client once described it. "The limbo has finally come to an end." They felt liberated.

The Blind Spot

The experience of dismissal is particularly painful when it catches the person completely off guard. This can be the case in situations of economic upheaval or takeovers, for example, when downsizing is taking place. However, it can also apply to dismissals that are specifically attributable to the person concerned— for performance reasons or repeated clashes with the corporate culture, for instance. While for everyone else the decision has long been on the horizon, the dismissed party suspects nothing. Their early warning system has failed.

One reason for this can be an exaggerated sense of self-esteem rooted in the person's attribution style. Attribution theories are used in psychology to explain how individuals perceive the causes of their everyday experi-ences. In this case, it could be that the person believed that the cause of the undesirable situation lay solely in their external circumstances. For this reason, they saw the cause as temporary and, moreover, restricted to a specific situation: *We've just got to get through this!* While such tenacity is a characteristic of resilience and can at times be an important managerial strength, it can lead to a blind spot if present to an excessive degree. The person concerned is unable to discern that they themselves could be the problem. This effect is intensified when there's an absence of feedback and criticism from those around them.

Overcoming the Emotional Slump

Once the shock of the dismissal has subsided, the first step is to process it emotionally. This is a major hurdle that you can overcome only by establishing the necessary separation between yourself and the job. Top managers and professionals, in particular, come to see their jobs as integral to their identities over time. At some point, they may regard themselves solely in terms of what's written on their business card or what they read about themselves in the newspaper. When they're laid off, not only does the job disappear, but their image of themselves is left in tatters. *What are the kids and neighbors going to think?* they wonder. This feeling is all the more potent the higher they climb on the career ladder.

I know of cases where the departing party faked the morning drive to work or the airport for weeks after the event to keep up appearances. Depending on the legal agreement and the financial settlement, their self-doubt may be compounded by financial worries and questions about whether they can maintain their current standard of living.

In this situation, it is essential for the person to talk to their spouse, friends, or perhaps a coach—someone who sees them not only as a board member or managing director but also as a human being.

Equally important is the need to look the truth in the face. While this might not be pleasant, accepting these uncomfortable feelings is precisely what's required for healing to begin. It would be misguided to try to avoid them; they're an integral part of the personal transformation process that has already been set in motion.

Avoiding False Starts

Those who have been let go from a job are in danger of falling into the "I'll show you" trap. After the crushing embarrassment of dismissal, it's only human that the desire for negative reparations in the form of "revenge" may arise. Unfortunately, this course of action is highly counterproductive. In pursuing it, the person shackles themselves mentally to the negative past event and leaves no spare capacity for a meaningful fresh start.

One typical mistake is to make a hasty switch to the competition, driven less by attractive career prospects than by the desire to show the old employer that the termination was a big mistake. Here, there's a danger that the competitor is interested only in poaching valuable knowledge and will drop the "defector" without a second thought once their usefulness is exhausted. In this case, the dismissal is set in stone before they begin. I know several clients and former colleagues who suffered this fate. In their case, the ostensible new start turned out to be a false one: they allowed themselves to be blinded by the instant gratification of (what they believed to be) redress. As a result, they were lured onto a road that went nowhere. Naturally, I also know of cases where the move to the competition worked out well. However, these cases all had something in common, namely that the next position and the one after that were agreed in advance and anchored in the contract. In my experience, this is the only way to ensure that a move to a competitor represents a real chance of returning to success.

One final word of caution: when you switch to the competition, it's always important to bear in mind that you will likely be irrevocably destroying bridges with your old employer. As a result, you may lose references for the further course of that career track.

A Powerful New Start

Rather than getting lost in rumination, it's crucial to take the following steps as soon as possible. It's not uncommon for a job search to take as long as nine to twelve months.

First, the departing party must reflect upon and understand the situation. This requires them to examine honestly the degree to which they contributed to the undesirable outcome and what they would do differently next time. It's also important to reflect on where their identity diverges from their reputation, since this is the best way to uncover blind spots. Honest and open feedback from former colleagues can help here.

> Only those who are prepared to reflect on their own behaviors, and not become preoccupied by the blame game, can successfully overcome professional setbacks and return to the path of success.

The next step is to clarify realistic goals and options moving forward. An equivalent position in another company? A move to another company at a lower level? Other career paths entirely? A move to a supervisory board position or a consulting role? Additional training? I have discussed these and other options with a number of clients over the years, so I know from experience how useful it is to cast the net as wide as possible. In my experience, there are three factors that determine the speed with which a fresh start is achieved. The first is the person's willingness to adjust their expectations and step down from their pedestal, accepting the fact that they are now an applicant and no longer the boss. This is something that some people find difficult.

The second factor is the person's ability to draw on their network. Of course, this can work only if they've carefully cultivated the network over years. Moreover, it is important to display tact and to consider the degree to which individual contacts may be reasonably called upon. As a consultant, I was always happy to help when a good client of mine found themselves looking for a job. However, I also received "emergency" calls from people I didn't know at all—those who had never even afforded me an appointment, let alone actually considered doing business with me. I could only assume that now, in their hour of need, my name had surfaced from a frantic review of their contacts. In these cases, I helped only when I happened to have time—and that was rarely the case.

Finally, it is important to be prepared for setbacks—or, put another way, to accept that it can take time for the right option to present itself again. For some job seekers, this is a few weeks; for others it's more than a year. But if there's one thing I can say with certainty, it's that in more than twenty years as a consultant and coach, I haven't known a single case in which someone didn't eventually find a satisfactory new position. Perhaps that can be a source of comfort.

Using Crises as Opportunities

The career setback experienced due to a layoff can be used as an opportunity for a bold new start. Those who are willing to accept and reflect on reality have a chance not only to overcome the crisis, but also to grow as people. As the following example shows, once they've overcome the crisis they may even find their life satisfaction is greater than it was before.

A client of mine, an executive in the chemical sector, had lost his position as CEO overnight. He had been personally blamed for a failed acquisition, and he'd never seen it coming. He used his forced time-out of more than twelve months to rethink his leadership style, his self-image, and his values. When he finally took up a new position, he appeared a changed man: relaxed and humorous. To ensure he kept his blind spot to a minimum in the future, he resolved to ask each member of his new leadership team two questions twice per year:

- In your view, which aspects of my behavior have strengthened the leadership team?
- Which aspects of my behavior have weakened it?

Before his personal crisis, it would have been unthinkable for him to ask his team for such feedback. He had used his painful experience to grow as a leader. Most importantly, his life satisfaction had increased. "This experience has been good for me," he told me. "I feel like I'm at peace within myself. I'm grounded again."

Exercise: An Ounce of Prevention Is Better Than a Pound of Cure

To ensure that you're equipped for an "emergency," take a deep dive into your network:

- Who in your network could assist you in the event of a job loss?
- How many recruiters do you have regular contact with?

If you don't already do so, make sure you obtain regular personal feedback. For tips, see the exercise "Actively Seeking Feedback" on page 69.

Turning the Corner: "Retirement" at the Next Exit on the Right!

"Sorry, this is my first retirement: I'm still practicing," says Heinrich Lohse to his wife in the Loriot comedy *Pappa Ante Portas*. Lohse, the fictional procurement manager of German pipe manufacturing company Deutsche Röhren AG, is forced to take early retirement after a comical error. The movie makes me cry with laughter every time I watch it. Yet the protagonist is a tragic hero who must master the most inevitable career challenge of all: the step from a meaningful leadership role into the "insignificance" of retirement. Only a small minority of executives succeed in executing this step without issue. Suffice it to say, Heinrich Lohse is not one of them—and this is precisely why there's so much to learn from him. Two lessons are particularly valuable: one, leave in good time, and two, don't take yourself too seriously afterward. I recommend the movie as a warm-up exercise for anyone starting to think about retirement themselves. There are special laws that govern the art of a successful new start in this phase of life.

"Life Thereafter"; or, The Third Life Phase

Even the most successful managers must, at some point, bid goodbye to their active careers and embrace retirement. Saying goodbye can be difficult, and the transition to the next phase of life even more so. The change is particularly manifest in the shift of daily rhythm and the loss of recognition, power, influence, and status. A sense of sudden insignificance creeps in; the ego takes a hit. A similar phenomenon is observed in professional athletes, some of whom suffer from mental health issues at the end of their sports careers and end up struggling with depression or addiction. They have become addicted to success. Ex–Formula 1 racer Alex Dias Ribeiro summed it up aptly when he said, "Unhappy is he who depends on success to be happy." To ensure that the "life thereafter" doesn't descend into great personal disappointment, it's important to prepare for it early on. Unfortunately, this preparation is usually neglected. The traditional model of a professional career distinguishes between three key life stages: education, work, and retirement. While in the first stage of life we prepare intensively, usually over two decades, for the second stage of life, we are rather more neglectful about preparing for the third stage. This is all the more regrettable on account of today's increased life expectancies: the third stage now holds more potential than ever. Research shows that children born in Western countries today have a 50 percent chance of living to be well over one hundred years old (Gratton and Scott 2016). Adjusted for the new life expectancy, this means that fifty will become the new forty and will fall in the middle of the period in which we typically start to fly high in our careers. As a result of higher life expectancy, new life phases are emerging: futurologists Peter Zellmann and Horst Opaschowski now speak of "five lives" (Opaschowski and Zellmann 2018). There's more than enough time, then, to start again—but it's crucial that we do so in the right way.

Start Planning Early

Each stage of life should "blossom," Hermann Hesse writes in his poem "Stufen" (Steps). To ensure that the third stage and those that follow are also rich in bloom, we must sow the seeds in good time. Anyone who is interested in supervisory board positions, advisory board positions, guest professorships, or consulting assignments cannot begin the search a mere two weeks before the farewell party. A good deal of advance planning and active networking is required, since these assignments don't materialize overnight. Those hoping to pursue a completely new direction should start their planning even earlier. To allow time for ideas to be developed, tested, and refined, it's advisable to begin planning at least five years before the exit date (see Hirt 2012, 216). Some managers start even earlier.

Consider a former consulting colleague, for example, who became a winemaker in his retirement. Today, he owns and runs a very successful winery in Piedmont. He bought the first piece of land in northern Italy—an abandoned vineyard—more than ten years before he retired as a consultancy partner. He subsequently added over fifty more plots and now farms over five hectares. He has turned a former hobby into his "new middle life."

He's not the only one. Since leaving her position as a managing director in the consumer goods sector, one of my clients has devoted her life to real estate and interior design—something she had pursued as a hobby for years prior. Other clients, meanwhile, are devoting their third stage of life to collecting art, studying history or mathematics as mature students, becoming coaches or mentors, or embarking on a spiritual path.

Over the years, all of these people allowed time and space for their passions to mature like a fine wine alongside their demanding jobs. Eventually they were able to make these passions the focus of their new middle life. In many cases, it was their passion that helped them step back at the right time.

By planning your exit early, you'll be prepared even if the departure comes sooner than expected. One of my clients was caught off guard when he was unexpectedly given early retirement. Though he was financially secure, he was far from being mentally prepared. Unfortunately, this led to mental health struggles. He never quite got over the involuntary departure. With early preparation, he could have avoided the worst of these effects.

Finding the Right Time to Go

"Those who are late will be punished by life itself," Mikhail Gorbachev is quoted as saying to Erich Honecker. We would do well to heed this wisdom when it comes to making a career exit. It is difficult to see once-successful executives miss their expiration dates and refuse to acknowledge that their time is up. They cling to their roles in spite of the fact that their decline has begun for all to see. Those who see few prospects for the third phase, in particular, are easily drawn into taking another spin on the carousel. They miss one exit after the next, diminishing their reputations all the while. Unfortunately, there have been many examples of this phenomenon among prominent leaders in politics and business. One who *did* make the jump in a timely fashion is former Siemens CEO Joe Kaeser, who spoke wisely in an interview of the "art of letting go" (Süddeutsche Zeitung 2020). Unfortunately, this is exactly what we don't learn at business school or in leadership seminars.

There is also a biological basis for the importance of letting go in time. Research shows that success and productivity increase on average in the first twenty years after the start of a career and decline thereafter (Simonton 1997). Accordingly, those who begin a career at age thirty will perform best at age fifty, then begin to achieve comparatively less. Entrepreneurs, on the other hand, reach their mental peak much earlier. According to *Harvard Business Review*, the majority of successful start-up founders are under the age of fifty (Frick 2014). Inventors and Nobel Prize winners typically have their greatest ideas even earlier, in their late thirties. This has to do with the different forms of intelligence humans possess.

A Different Perspective on the Third Phase

In psychology, we distinguish between fluid and crystalline intelligence. This form of classification is attributed to the British-American personality psychologist Raymond Cattell (Cattell 1943). *Fluid intelligence* is the ability to think logically, analyze, and solve new problems. It is the type of intelligence we typically attribute to innovators and inventors. Fluid intelligence peaks in early adulthood and declines after age thirty—which explains, for example, the young average age of successful start-up entrepreneurs. *Crystalline intelligence*, on the other hand, is the ability to use experience and knowledge. It is what we commonly understand as wisdom.

Psychology suggests that, in older age, it is worthwhile to focus on tasks connected to the passing on of knowledge, such as teaching, mediating, and personal consulting. By doing so, we focus on the strengths that not only persist but continue to increase over the years.

Of course, this doesn't mean that starting a business is off-limits in older age. On the contrary: there are many successful start-ups by so-called *encore* entrepreneurs, those who become founders later in life, often over the age of fifty. This was the case with one of my clients. Instead of trying his hand at high-tech entrepreneurship, he founded a social enterprise and now builds and operates daycare centers for children. In another example, a former partner colleague of mine founded a nonprofit platform that matches factory-new in-kind donations to nonprofit organizations based on need. For many people at this stage of life, it's all about giving back. Fortunately, this goal is wonderfully compatible with our abilities as we age.

Finding Meaning and Happiness in the Third Phase

Some years ago, an Indian client and I shared an illuminating conversation on the third phase. I was working with a steel manufacturer at the time and traveling a lot in India. He told me about *vānaprastha*, the phase of life between the ages of fifty and seventy-five—what the West calls retirement. In Hinduism, vānaprastha refers to letting go of earthly rewards like money, power, and prestige and discovering our true selves. In the past, we would have adopted a rather stereotypical understanding of such a mandate: retiring to the forest, perhaps, and practicing yoga and meditation to gain spiritual clarity. Today, it can mean something much more nuanced. We might cease to focus exclusively on professional ambitions and, at the same time, adjust our life goals and devote more time to spiritual matters and wisdom. My former client has since retired from his profession and now works for a nonprofit organization, following the call of his religion and philosophy.

The more we imbue the third phase of life with meaning, the more happiness we will feel. After the age of fifty, happiness is on our side anyway. In his book *The Happiness Curve*, journalist Jonathan Rauch shows that our experience of happiness progresses like a U-shaped curve (Rauch 2018). Over the course of our careers, our sense of happiness steadily decreases; as we age, typically after age fifty, it increases again. The U-curve can be explained by our expectations. When we're young, we are overly optimistic and overestimate the life satisfaction we'll have in the future. We are often disappointed. In older age, our life satisfaction remains constant, but our expectations are lower. Relatively speaking, our sense of happiness is increased. Not only are we well equipped to pursue a new role in society—one that goes far beyond competition and individual ambition—we can also look forward to one of the most content and tranquil phases of human life.

Preparing for the Jump

Generally speaking, the optimal time to leave is when we have achieved all of our professional goals and still feel that we have energy for more. We need to anticipate when this moment will come—and this requires effective preparation.

Before beginning the actual planning, I have found it can be helpful to search for a metaphor as a guiding principle for the third phase of life. Wolfgang did exactly this in our case study. A metaphor is a representative symbol, a picture that helps us visualize our goal beyond abstract concepts and bring it to mind whenever we need to. In my work with coaching clients, I have encountered a number of metaphors for the third phase of life. There has been talk of a personal renaissance, the end of the rodeo, the completion of one's life painting, a milestone, opening up, and arriving. As you approach the third phase, it's worthwhile to find a metaphor of your own.

The next step involves developing a personal strategic plan, preferably by focusing on the following three questions:

- Where am I?
- Where do I want to get to?
- How will I get there?

The inclusion of three time horizons in this process is deliberate: as discussed, the third phase of life is often no longer our last. You can use the following structure to help you develop your personal strategic plan in more detail.

Where am I?	Where do I want to get to?		How will I get there?
	In five years?	In ten years?	What will I do? When? Who will help me?

Work

Family and friends

Hobbies

Personal development

My metaphor

Your personal development plan

Exercise: Your Personal Development Plan

Find your personal metaphor for the third phase and create your personal development plan. Get started right away.

In a nutshell:

- It can pay to take a career break. However, start your preparations to return early, especially if you've spent a long time away from work.
- For career breaks lasting up to six months, the return to work is usually quite straightforward.
- In the case of involuntary time off due to job loss, first focus on mindfully working through the mental slump. Avoid reflexive emotional reactions.
- A job loss offers you the opportunity to make a powerful new start, provided you use the time to reflect and properly process the personal crisis.
- Making the jump to the third phase at the right time is the key to opening up a vast array of options. You'll have the chance to embark on a new start and to make a difference.
- Begin planning for the third phase at least five years before your planned exit.

For the Curious among You: Where Wolfgang Is Now

Retirement never really got off the ground for Wolfgang; it was more of a temporary break. Now, in his third phase of life, Wolfgang is enjoying a flying new start. He has collaborated with his friends to build a platform specializing in impact investments—those that aim to have positive social and ecological effects in addition to a financial return. This could be anything from environmental issues to education. The platform is financing numerous start-ups and has partnered with numerous prestigious companies from the fields of law and financing. Similarly, the mentor network has recruited a number of respected business personalities. In our last session, Wolfgang reported that he was completely satisfied. He has not yet written his memoirs, though, so you'll have to wait for his catchily titled book!

Success Gone on Vacation? Don't Worry: It's Okay

"Where are you going with that big backpack, anyway?" the woman asked me, pausing briefly from cursing the disappearance of her scanner card. She was running a small courier service from her apartment in Cologne, and I'd stopped by to drop off a parcel. She placed it on a large pile in the corner.

"I'm hiking to Munich," I replied.

She was almost speechless. "And you're passing by here, in Cologne?"

Five days prior, I had said goodbye to my job as a senior partner at Boston Consulting Group and set out on my long-distance trek from Düsseldorf to Munich. It was the perfect time for a break before moving on to my next professional chapter. I wanted to get away from it all, thoughts of success included. Over the last twenty years, I'd flown the route on countless occasions for client appointments and internal meetings. I'd made the journey so often that I'd long since given up counting the number of times. On one of the flights, I was struck by the idea of walking the route. The flight takes just an hour; for my hike, I had set aside four weeks. Two days before, I had packed my backpack, said goodbye to my family, and simply started walking, to the end of town and then along the next dirt road.

I had only a rough idea of my route. Cologne, Westerwald, Taunus, Frankfurt, Odenwald, Swabian Alb, the Alpine foothills, and finally Munich: these were the milestone points I had in mind. There was no guidebook for this route, and there were few other walkers—certainly not in COVID times. It was just a few days prior that guesthouses and hotels had reopened to tourism in a small number of federal states. As a result, I wasn't sure if I would find accommodation in all the places I needed. I only ever used my hiking app to plan three days in advance; the rest, I thought, could be figured out in time. Four weeks without firm plans was a test for a consultant like me. I thought of Franz Kafka, who was believed to have said, "Paths are made by walking."

It was for other reasons besides the lack of plans that the hike had proved an interesting exercise thus far. For some reason, I had decided to set off with hiking boots that were more than ten years old. It took only until the second day to realize my mistake: 10 kilometers before Cologne, the soles of my shoes came loose. *Signs of fatigue,* I thought. *My trusty hiking companions probably aren't quite up to it anymore.* With some difficulty, I carried out makeshift repairs with a piece of string and made my way to the next outdoor store in Cologne, where I bought a new pair. The old ones, which I couldn't bear to part with, would be returning home via the package I had dropped off. Breaking in the shoes meant a tough few days. *If only I'd parted with the old ones earlier,* I thought, *I could have spared myself all of this.* It was a painful reminder of the importance of letting go at the right time, for which my hiking boots became a kind of metaphor.

Google Maps states that the walking route between my front door in Meerbusch, close to Düsseldorf, and the Marienplatz in Munich is 560 kilometers long. Realistically, it is more like 780 kilometers—assuming, as a friend jokingly remarked to me, that you wouldn't necessarily want to hike along the A3 highway. Among other sights, it takes in the Via Publica, a now-inconspicuous country lane that began as one of the main eighteenth-century European transport routes. The route then proceeds along the Limes and the Way of St. James, through suburbs whose streets are lined with one gym after the next, and through wonderful little villages whose names I'd never heard of before. Apart from telephone conversations with my family, the only people I spoke to were the proprietors of the guesthouses where I stayed. We talked in the evening over a glass of beer. On three occasions I was not just the only guest but probably also the last. These establishments were being forced to close down for good. Success here meant merely surviving, which was made all the harder in COVID times.

My path led me further and further southward. I walked along poker-straight paths through endless forests, on narrow paths through rolling hills, through areas that were as primitive as primeval jungles. When I entered the forests, the birds greeted me by chirping and bid me farewell when I stepped back into the open. I spent a few days walking with my wife, who met me on the route for a long weekend. This was a highlight. Otherwise, I spent quiet days advancing on my way. Only twice did I meet other long-distance hikers, among them a couple heading north, armed only with a compass. A pilgrim on the Way of St. James provided a rave review of his state-of-the-art trekking equipment. Most of the time, I was shrouded in silence. It was a silence I had not expected; I was in the middle of Germany, after all.

In my head, though, I found little silence at first. Though I had resolved not to think about professional matters, I spent the first week doing exactly that. I checked my smartphone eagerly and read personal messages about my departure from the firm. I found myself calculating the average kilometers per day required to cover the distance in four weeks. A typical consultant, I know. But with each passing day, I became more at one with my hike and began to see the world a little differently. I got up in the morning and walked, open to what the day would bring. I had no expectations. Again and again, small surprises revealed themselves: a magnificent view, a beer garden, a small but charming chapel. In addition, the hiking was becoming easier. I was covering daily distances of almost 40 kilometers with no more effort than it took to sit on a plane.

I turned off my phone during the day and used it only in the evenings to call my family. The text messages dwindled over time; my mailbox was empty. I experienced feelings of freedom, lightness, and happiness. Whenever I was hiking, I was completely in the present; I attained a wonderful state of mental clarity. For the first time, I was mindful of the diversity of the flora and fauna and the brilliant blue of the sky. I couldn't get enough of it: Why had I never noticed it before? I felt an emptiness and inner stillness almost like that attained in meditation. It was like I was existing between two worlds; I had left the old one but not yet entered the new. Every thought of professional success had vanished. I wandered south for almost three weeks, oblivious to the passage of time.

Three days before I arrived in Munich, I received an unexpected phone call in the evening. The CEO of a mechanical engineering company—someone I'd never met before—was on the line. He had heard in a roundabout way that I was now working as an executive coach, and he wanted to engage me for a major assignment with the board. There it was once more—the reminder of professional success—as if it had been waiting for me at the end of the road. *Welcome to your new life*, it said. When I arrived at Marienplatz in Munich after thirty days of walking, my first big coaching job was already in the bag.

Again, I had learned something: it's okay not to be successful for a while. On the contrary, it's nice to meet success again afterward, well refreshed for the road ahead.

Epilogue: My Own Case Study

How on earth does someone who studied the technical feasibility of comet missions end up becoming an executive coach? Did I take a wrong turn? In reality, it was more that I simply kept driving: I didn't pay attention to the signs at all. My journey has taken me from the Oort cloud—deep in the far reaches of space—to the inner galaxies of executive personality types. While there was no map for this route in the neighborhood bookstore, the route itself was not exactly the problem. What was more challenging was that my engine for success had a tendency to stutter from time to time. At these times, I would have liked to have a manual to refer to.

Eventually, I came to realize that the simple maintenance manual I was looking for—the type designed for cars, luggage, and everything in between—didn't exist. This is why I've written my own manual, for all those who are still on the road. It's based on experiences gathered over a many-year journey. In retrospect, I probably had to complete this journey in order to be able to write it at all. With this in mind, it feels apt to conclude the book with my own case study.

The "Savior of German Mechanical Engineering"

It never once occurred to me that I would end up writing a book about success. I hardly ever read books when I was young: my collection consisted solely of an activity manual called *The Crafting Book for Boys.* "It looks a little lonely up there on your shelf," a friend told me, handing me the Rolling Stones biography. Then, I had two books; today, I have a passable collection. Admittedly, I was a late starter when it came to reading—and the same could be said for my ambitions regarding success and career. School and grades were of secondary importance, my high school diploma was mediocre, and my studies in aerospace engineering at the Technical University of Braunschweig were only half-hearted at first. I dreamed instead of making it with one of my rock bands. At the time, I earned money on the side drumming for dance bands at various *Schützenfesten*, traditional German village festivals. It was a dark chapter. At some point, I realized it was not my destiny to make it onto the cover of *Rolling Stone* magazine. I resolved to focus on my second passion, engineering. I stepped up a gear in my studies.

I couldn't have picked a worse time to enter the world of work: It was 1993 and the export trade was sluggish. Opportunities for engineers in the job market were poor, and for the most part, getting a job as a new graduate was a matter of pure luck. Still, I sent unsolicited applications with a creative cover letter and, after a short time, received an invitation for a first interview. As I entered the room, I was greeted by resounding laughter and an allusion to the letter's opening line: "Look, there he is—the savior of German mechanical engineering!" As it turned out, this self-proclaimed title had won me the job—as a sales and application engineer at a specialist mechanical engineering company in Duisburg called Mannesmann Demag AG. I felt proud and happy as I signed the employment contract. Perhaps most importantly, I had learned that it sometimes takes a little courage to get results.

It was an exciting job involving global travel: London, Paris, Rio, Delhi, Trinidad. The business was flourishing. I soon took on my first leadership role: responsibility for a newly created product team who would develop and launch a new range of machines. Our team reported directly to the technical board. We were nicknamed *Jugend forscht* ("Youth researches")—an allusion to a well-known German science education foundation—as a nod to the fact that it was previously unheard of for young employees to enjoy so much autonomy. Sales, project management, engineering, purchasing, manufacturing, commissioning: all of it was up to us. It was like being in a start-up. It allowed me to uncover a side of myself that had been previously hidden: my secret inner entrepreneur.

The Bumpy Road to the World of Management Consulting

Our team was successful. Probably because of this, I was given the chance to spend a year in France doing an MBA at the *École des Affaires Paris*, or EAP (now *École Supérieure de Commerce de Paris*, or ESCP). This period was a turning point: I learned a great deal about strategy, management, organization, and leadership. Perhaps more importantly, I got to meet new and different people: investment bankers, marketing experts, even musicians. New possibilities blossomed before me, for the rest of my career and the rest of my life. For the first time, I toyed with the idea of becoming a management consultant. Might I even have what it took to make it to the major leagues? I had received an invitation to interview with Boston Consulting Group (BCG). Though it felt like an opportunity too good to miss, my final decision was to turn it down.

Instead, I went back to Mannesmann, where I had been offered the chance to manage a new business segment. It was a big career jump: I became the poster child for promotion opportunities within the group. I had international responsibility for four large teams consisting of experienced engineers and businesspeople, whose remit was to work on complex special machinery projects for specialty chemicals. I learned a lot about leadership, not least the fact that things are very different when you lead just one team compared to several. In theory, I should have been satisfied. Yet when I had made the decision to return, there was one factor that I had overlooked: in Paris, I had seen and come to appreciate a very different type of world. Back at Mannesmann, everything suddenly felt rather rigid. As exciting as my promotion sounded on paper, in practice, I was dealing with the same customers and problems day in, day out. Had I made a mistake? As I tried to untangle things, something happened that changed everything.

The Mannesmann conglomerate was taken over by Vodafone—one of the largest corporate takeovers in the history of the Federal Republic of

Germany to date. Everything that wasn't part of mobile communications was divested. Unwilling to simply wait to see where I would wash up like driftwood, I took the reins: I called BCG and, some two and a half years after the initial invitation, I informed them that I would accept the interview. In truth, I wasn't a typical fit—in age or grades—for BCG's target candidates. A consultant had already informed me of that. But when I received an offer, I realized again what's possible when you follow your dreams—albeit in my case, there had been a detour along the way. I had the feeling that I was on the winning track.

The BCG Matrix and the Iron-Carbon Diagram

Unfortunately, I had underestimated the difficulty of the transition from experienced engineer to rank beginner in a new field. For me, this was a tough period that pushed me to my mental limits. I found myself trapped between two worlds, with one foot in the door at BCG and the other still—mentally—at Mannesmann. I knew what I had given up, but not yet what I would get in return, apart from the long workdays and little time for my family. I increasingly had the feeling that I had once again made a mistake. At the same time, I learned a lot about myself and how important it is to let go in a transition phase. It was only when I succeeded in doing this that my first successes began to materialize.

After two years, I became involved in a reorganization project for a steel manufacturer. Suddenly the impasse seemed to be broken: I understood how consulting worked and was able to use my technical background to boot. My ability to switch from the BCG matrix to the iron-carbon diagram with equal aplomb appealed to our rather technical-minded customer. In addition, my industry and leadership experience gave me credibility as a consultant. I had found my niche and ascended through the ranks: from consultant to project leader and from there to principal. With that came an additional offer to take on the role of recruiting director. From then on, I wore two hats: one for my clients and one for BCG recruiting. Later, I wore a third hat for internal career development. I had discovered a new passion in myself: helping others on their career path. I had reached the next turning point.

After seven and a half years at BCG, I was elected partner. I felt as though I had crossed the finish line of a marathon, and I was suitably proud to have made it. I didn't realize, however, that this step had also changed the laws for success. From then on, I had to sell consulting projects and establish contacts instead of delving into technical analyses. Not surprisingly, I didn't succeed at first. The transition was challenging in all the same ways as last time. Once again, I had to learn to let go of my old role and, at the same time, to fight an inner adversary. This was one of the most difficult periods of my professional life. Later, the highly experienced coach who assisted me with this transition became my role model for getting into coaching myself.

A New Perspective

It was around that time that I also came to find out about Zen meditation. Prompted by an unusual experience in a monastery in South Korea, I began to engage with the subject in depth. I became more relaxed, gained new vitality, and was able to gain new perspective on my life. Change yourself and everything around you will change, Zen teaches us. Indeed, as I changed myself, a lot began to change. Suddenly I was achieving business success in my partner role and assumed leadership of a practice group in Europe. Around the same time, I started training as an executive coach at Meyler Campbell in London. These twin challenges were tricky to reconcile, including for my family. I sensed that they also marked the next big turning point. In reality, I wasn't quite that far yet.

Our practice group had progressed very well in Europe, and in the meantime, I had ascended to senior partner. I was offered global responsibility for the practice group, an offer I was hesitant to accept at first. I had too great a respect for the prestige of the top ranks, and I was worried that I would have to travel even more often. Eventually, though, I went ahead. Looking back, it was the right decision. I was working with a large international team, digitalization was giving our business an unexpected boost, and we were the first practice group in BCG's history to exceed the magic revenue mark of $1 billion. As a practice group leader, I also sat on the central committees for personnel development for all partners worldwide.

I had taken a risk, and things couldn't have gone better. This, too, was an important learning experience. At the same time, I had the sense that my consulting journey was slowly coming to its natural end. An inner voice was speaking up once again.

A Warning Shot with Far-Reaching Ripples: The Path to Becoming a Coach

Amidst all these exciting developments, I had completed my training as a coach and, in parallel with my work at BCG, had begun to experiment with my first coaching assignments. I discovered that not only did I enjoy this work immensely, but it energized me in a way I hadn't felt for a while. A third factor also came into play: my desire to become self-employed and to own something of my own once again. Sadly, it was the unexpected death of a friend and colleague that was the catalyst for my final decision. The two of us had often sat together at lunch and philosophized about what we would do after BCG. Now, he had been denied the chance to experience it. It was like a warning shot: I pulled the rip cord and quit.

Funnily enough, my departure from BCG coincided with the beginning of the COVID crisis. It was a strange confluence of events that caused bemusement among my colleagues at first. "Tell us: how did you know about COVID?" a colleague joked at the farewell celebration on my final day. In retrospect, I believe I quit at exactly the right time—not, though, because of the pandemic. I had worked for what I considered to be one of the best companies in the world, achieved more than I could ever have hoped, and—crucially—still had the drive to pursue something new. This time, I would be a coach, entrepreneur, and author. The transition went smoothly. My engine for success is already up and running and my business is on a steep upward curve.

Who knows, maybe this book will mark the next turning point.

References

Allrecht Rechtsschutzversicherungen. 2019. *Sabbatical-Modelle.
So können Mitarbeiter eine Auszeit nehmen.* October 9, 2019.
https://www.allrecht.de/alles-was-recht-ist/sabbatical-modelle/.

Amabile, Teresa, and Steven Kramer. 2011. *The Progress Principle: Using
Small Wins to Ignite Joy, Engagement and Creativity at Work.* Boston:
Harvard Business Review Press.

Bacon, Francis. 2017. *Neues Organon. Große Erneuerung der Wissen-
schaften.* Berlin: Verlag der Contumax GmbH & Co. KG.

Berne, Eric. 2019. *Spiele der Erwachsenen. Psychologie der menschlichen
Beziehungen.* 20th ed. Hamburg: Rowohlt Taschenbuch Verlag.

Boston Consulting Group. 2019. Keine Lust mehr auf Führungsverantwortung.
Manager Magazin. September 21, 2019. https://www.manager-magazin
.de/unternehmen/artikel/boston-consulting-group-fuehrung-unter
-mitarbeitern-nicht-mehr-gefragt-a-1287950.html.

Boyatzis, Richard, Melvin Smith, and Ellen Van Oosten. 2019. *Helping
People Change: Coaching with Compassion for Lifelong Learning and
Growth.* Boston: Harvard Business Review Press.

Branson, Richard. 2014. "You Can't Succeed in Business without Making
Personal Connections." *Canadian Business.* February 6, 2014.

Bridges, William, and Susan Bridges. 2018. *Managing Transitions. Erfolgreich
durch Übergänge und Veränderungsprozesse führen.* 4th ed. Munich:
Verlag Franz Vahlen.

Buckingham, Marcus, and Donald O. Clifton. 2016. *Entdecken Sie Ihre
Stärken jetzt! Das Gallup-Prinzip für individuelle Entwicklung und
erfolgreiche Führung.* 5th ed. Frankfurt: Campus Verlag.

Cappuccio, Francesco P., Lanfranco D'Elia, Pasquale Strazzullo, and Michelle
A. Miller. 2010. "Sleep Duration and All-Cause Mortality: A Systematic
Review and Meta-Analysis of Prospective Studies." *Sleep* 33, no. 5 (May):
585–92. https://doi.org/10.1093/sleep/33.5.585.

Cattell, Raymond. 1943. "The Measurement of Adult Intelligence." *Psychological Bulletin* 40, no. 3 (March): 153–93. https://doi.org/10.1037 /h0059973.

Charan, Ram, Stephen Drotter, and James Noel. 2001. *The Leadership Pipeline: How to Build the Leadership-Powered Company.* San Francisco: Jossey-Bass.

Clear, James. 2020. *Die 1%-Methode—Minimale Veränderung, maximale Wirkung. Mit kleinen Gewohnheiten jedes Ziel erreichen.* 11th ed. Munich: Goldmann Verlag.

Collins, Jim. 2001. *Good to Great: Why Some Companies Make the Leap and Others Don't.* New York: Random House.

Covey, Stephen R., A. Roger Merrill, and Rebecca R. Merrill. 1994. *First Things First.* New York: Simon & Schuster.

Dalio, Ray. 2019. *Die Prinzipien des Erfolgs: Bridgewater-Gründer Ray Dalios Principles mit dem Prinzip der stetigen Verbesserung.* Munich: FinanzBuch Verlag.

Damasio, Antonio R. 2004. *Descartes' Irrtum. Fühlen, Denken und das menschliche Gehirn.* Berlin: Ullstein Verlag.

David, Susan. 2016. *Emotional Agility. Get Unstuck, Embrace Change and Thrive in Work and Life.* New York: Penguin Random House.

De Smet, Aaron, Bonnie Dowling, Marino Mugayar-Baldocchi, and Bill Schaninger. 2021. "Great Attrition or Great Attraction? The Choice Is Yours." *McKinsey Quarterly.* September 8, 2021. https://www.mckinsey .com/business-functions/people-and-organizational-performance/our -insights/great-attrition-or-great-attraction-the-choice-is-yours.

Duhigg, Charles. 2013. *Die Macht der Gewohnheit. Warum wir tun, was wir tun.* 9th ed. Munich: Piper Verlag.

Dürckheim, Karlfried Graf. 2012. *Hara. Die energetische Mitte des Menschen.* Munich: O.W. Barth Verlag.

Dweck, Carol. 2017. *Selbstbild. Wie unser Denken Erfolge oder Niederlagen bewirkt.* 5th ed. Translated by Jürgen Neubauer. Munich: Piper Verlag.

Ekman, Paul. 2010. *Gefühle lesen. Wie Sie Emotionen erkennen und richtig interpretieren.* 2nd ed. Heidelberg: Spektrum Akademischer Verlag.

Ensser, Michael, ed. 2014. *Connecting Leaders—Dialogue.* Zurich: Egon Zehnder International Inc.

Ericsson, Anders, and Robert Pool. 2017. *Peak: Secrets from the New Science of Expertise.* Boston: Mariner Books.

Etzold, Veit. 2020. *Wandel kommunizieren.* Offenbach, Germany: GABAL Verlag.

Ferriss, Timothy. 2015. *Die 4-Stunden-Woche. Mehr Zeit, mehr Geld, mehr Leben.* 12th ed. Berlin: Ullstein Verlag.

Founders Circle Capital. 2022. *In the Front Door, Out the Back: Attrition Challenges at High Growth Startups.* https://www.founderscircle.com /high-startup-turnover-rate.

Frick, Walter. 2014. "How Old are Silicon Valley's Top Founders? Here's the Data." *Harvard Business Review.* April 3, 2014. https://hbr.org /2014/04/how-old-are-silicon-valleys-top-founders-heres-the-data.

Gallwey, Timothy. 1986. *The Inner Game of Tennis.* London: Pan Books.

Gerhuasen, Petra, and Angela Baumgarten. 2021. *Neuwagenkauf–Tipps für die Probefahrt.* ADAC. July 1, 2021. https://www.adac.de/rund-ums -fahrzeug/auto-kaufen-verkaufen/neuwagenkauf/vor-dem-kauf/.

Gladwell, Malcolm. 2001. *The Tipping Point: How Little Things Can Make a Big Difference.* Boston: Little, Brown and Company.

Goldsmith, Marshall. 2007. *What Got You Here Won't Get You There: How Successful People Become Even More Successful.* New York: Hyperion Books.

Goleman, Daniel. 1997. *Emotionale Intelligenz–EQ.* Munich: Deutscher Taschenbuch Verlag.

Goleman, Daniel. 2022. Emotionale Intelligenz. *Harvard Business Manager, Spezial 2022.*

Gratton, Lynda, and Andrew Scott. 2016. *The 100-Year Life: Living and Working in an Age of Longevity.* London: Bloomsbury Information.

Grawe, Klaus. 2012. *Neuropsychotherapie.* Göttingen, Germany: Hogrefe Verlag.

Greiser, Christian, and Jan-Philipp Martini. 2018. "How Companies Can Instill Mindfulness." *Knowledge@Wharton.* April 19, 2018. https:// knowledge.wharton.upenn.edu/article/how-companies-can-instill -mindfulness/.

Groysberg, Boris. 2012. *Chasing Stars: The Myth of Talent and the Portability of Performance.* Princeton, NJ: Princeton University Press.

Gutefrage.net. 2017. *Darf man beim Motorrad neues Öl einfach dazu füllen, ohne das alte abzulassen?* April 5, 2017. https://www.gutefrage.net /frage/darf-man-beim-motorrad-neues-oel-einfach-dazu-fuellen-ohne -das-alte-abzulassen.

Haidt, Jonathan. 2006. *The Happiness Hypothesis: Finding Modern Truth in Ancient Wisdom*. New York: Basic Books.

Heath, Fred (Chip), and Jeffrey (Dan) Heath. 2013. *Switch. Veränderungen wagen und dadurch gewinnen.* 5th ed. Berlin: Fischer Taschenbuch Verlag.

Hirt, Michael. 2012. *Das CEO-Handbuch. Optimal vorbereitet für Ihre Position an der Spitze.* Zürich: vdf Hochschulverlag an der ETH Zürich.

Hogan, Robert, and Robert B. Kaiser. 2005. "What We Know About Leadership." *Review of General Psychology* 9, no. 2 (June): 169–80. https://doi.org/10.1037/1089-2680.9.2.169.

Huffington, Arianna. 2014. *Die Neuerfindung des Erfolgs. Weisheit, Staunen, Großzügigkeit. Was uns wirklich weiter bringt.* Gütersloh, Germany: Riemann Verlag.

Ibarra, Herminia. 2002. *Working Identity. Unconventional Strategies for Reinventing Your Career.* Boston: Harvard Business School Press.

Ibarra, Herminia. 2015. "The Authenticity Paradox." *Harvard Business Review.* Jan/Feb 2015. https://hbr.org/2015/01/the-authenticity-paradox.

Iso-Ahola, Seppo, and Charles Dotson. 1986. "Psychological Momentum and Competitive Sports: A Field Study." *Perceptual and Motor Skills* 62, no. 3 (June): 763–68. https://doi.org/10.2466/pms.1986.62.3.763.

Johnson, Whitney. 2019. *Disrupt Yourself. Master Relentless Change and Speed Up Your Learning Curve (Illustrated Edition).* Boston: Harvard Business Review Press.

Kahneman, Daniel. 2011. *Schnelles Denken, langsames Denken.* 19th ed. Translated by Thorsten Schmidt. Munich: Siedler Verlag.

Keirsey, David. 1998. *Please Understand Me II: Temperament, Character, Intelligence.* Wilmington, DE: Prometheus Nemesis Book Company.

Kerkeling, Hape. 2006. *Ich bin dann mal weg. Meine Reise auf dem Jakobsweg.* Munich: Piper Verlag.

Kerler, Richard, and Peter von Windau. 1992. *Die 100 Gesetze erfolgreicher Karriereplanung.* Berlin: Ullstein Verlag.

Kleitman, Nathaniel. 1982. "Basic Rest-Activity Cycle—22 Years Later." *Sleep* 5, no. 4 (September), 311–17. https://doi.org/10.1093/sleep/5.4.311.

Kline, Nancy. 1999. *Time to Think. Listening to Ignite the Human Mind.* London: Cassell Illustrated.

Klüver, Nathalie. 2016. *Frauen im Beruf: Willkommen am Karriereknick. Interview mit Soziologe Fabian Ochsenfeld.* Unicum Karrierezentrum. February 16, 2016.

Leslie, Jean Brittain, and Ellen van Velsor. 1996. "A Look at Derailment Today." Greensboro, NC: Center for Creative Leadership.

Lorenz, Thomas, and Stefan Oppitz. 2015. *30 Minutes to Enhance Your Profile through Personality: On the Basis of the Myers-Briggs Type Indicator (MBTI)*. 3rd ed. Offenbach, Germany: GABAL Verlag.

Matthes, Sebastian, and Christian Rickens. 2021. Interview with Arianna Huffington: "Ein guter Morgen beginnt am Abend zuvor". *Handelsblatt*. May 28, 2021. https://www.handelsblatt.com/unternehmen /management/interview-arianna-huffington-ein-guter-morgen-beginnt -am-abend-zuvor/27227904.html.

Meister, Jeanne. 2012. "The Future of Work: Job Hopping Is the 'New Normal' for Millennials." *Forbes*. August 14, 2012. https://www.forbes.com /sites/jeannemeister/2012/08/14/the-future-of-work-job-hopping-is-the -new-normal-for-millennials/?sh=4a8d219113b8.

Microsoft. 2021. "The Next Great Disruption Is Hybrid Work. Are We Ready?" March 22, 2021. https://www.microsoft.com/en-us/worklab /work-trend-index/hybrid-work.

Mulisch, Harry, and Peter Saalbach. 1999. Man muss ablernen. In Heinrich Von Pierer and Bolko von Oetinger, *Wie kommt das Neue in die Welt?* Hamburg: Rowohlt Taschenbuch Verlag.

nw. 2022. *Bei Motorüberhitzung besteht akuter Handlungsbedarf!* Autofahrerseite.EU. https://autofahrerseite.eu/tipps-trends/520-bei -motorueberhitzung-besteht-akuter-handlungsbedarf.html.

OECD. 2019. *Die Zukunft der Arbeit. OECD-Beschäftigungsausblick 2019*. https:// www.oecd.org/employment/Employment-Outlook-2019-Highlight-DE.pdf.

Opaschowski, Horst, and Peter Zellmann. 2018. *Du hast fünf Leben!* Vienna: Manz Verlag.

Pascale, Richard, Mark Millemann, and Linda Gioja. 2000. *Surfing the Edge of Chaos: The Laws of Nature and the New Laws of Business*. New York: Three Rivers Press.

Peters, Tom. 2002. *This I believe! Tom's 60 TIBs. An Excerpt from Project 04. Snapshots of Excellence in Unstable Times*. https://tompeters.com /blogs/freestuff/uploads/2.01.ThisIBelieve.pdf.

Porter, Michael E., and Nitin Nohria. 2018. "How CEOs Manage Time." *Harvard Business Review Magazine* (July–August 2018). https://hbr.org /2018/07/how-ceos-manage-time.

Rauch, Jonathan. 2018. *The Happiness Curve: Why Life Gets Better after Midlife*. London: Green Tree.

Ries, Eric. 2012. *Lean Startup. Schnell, risikolos und erfolgreich Unternehmen gründen.* Translated by Ursula Bischoff. Munich: Redline Verlag.

Schootstra, Emma, Dirk Deichmann, and Evgenia Dolgova. 2017. "Can 10 Minutes of Meditation Make You More Creative?" *Harvard Business Review.* August 29, 2017. https://hbr.org/2017/08/can-10-minutes-of -meditation-make-you-more-creative.

Seligman, Martin E. P. 2005. *Der Glücksfaktor. Warum Optimisten länger leben.* 16th ed. Cologne, Germany: Bastei Lübbe.

Simonton, Dean Keith. 1997. "Creative Productivity. A Predictive and Explanatory Model of Career Trajectories and Landmarks." *Psychological Review* 104, no. 1 (January): 66–89. https://doi.org/10.1037/0033-295X.104.1.66.

Sinek, Simon. 2014. *Frag immer erst: warum. Wie Topfirmen und Führungskräfte zum Erfolg inspirieren.* Munich: Redline Verlag.

Statista. 2017. *Sabbatical. Einfach mal Pause machen.* January 19, 2017. https://de.statista.com/infografik/amp/7663/einstellung-der-deutschen -arbeitnehmer-zum-sabbatical/.

Statistisches Bundesamt. 2019. *Qualität der Arbeit. Personen in Elternzeit.* https://www.destatis.de/DE/Themen/Arbeit/Arbeitsmarkt/Qualitaet -Arbeit/Dimension-3/elternzeit.html.

Strogatz, Steven H. 2003. *Sync: How Order Emerges from Chaos in the Universe, Nature, and Daily Life.* New York: Hyperion Books.

Süddeutsche Zeitung. 2020. Der bessere Chef. *Süddeutsche Zeitung.* December 18, 2020. https://www.sueddeutsche.de/wirtschaft /siemens-joe-kaeser-nachfol-ger-roland-busch-1.5152779.

Sull, Donald, Charles Sull, and Ben Zweig. 2022. "Toxic Culture Is Driving the Great Resignation." *MIT SLOAN Management Review.* January 11, 2022. https://sloanreview.mit.edu/article/toxic-culture-is-driving-the -great-resignation/.

Suzuki, Shunryu. 1999. *Zen-Geist, Anfänger-Geist. Unterweisungen in Zen-Meditation.* Bielefeld, Germany: Theseus Verlag.

Tan, Chade-Meng. 2012. *Search Inside Yourself. Das etwas andere Glücks-Coaching.* New York: Arkana.

Thaler, Richard H., and Cass R. Sunstein. 2017. *Nudge. Wie man kluge Entscheidungen anstößt* 7th ed. Berlin: Ullstein Verlag.

Theophil, Andre. 2019. *Zündkerzen wechseln. Damit der Funke überspringt.* Auto Bild. November 11, 2019. https://www.autobild.de/artikel /zuendkerzen-wechseln-10507957.html#anchor_1.

Theophil, Andre, Stefan Novitsky, and Lena Trautermann. 2022. *Die Motorkontrollleuchte leuchtet auf? Das ist zu tun.* Auto Bild. July 14, 2022. https://www.autobild.de/artikel/motorkontrollleuchte-darum -leuchtet-oder-blinkt-die-mkl-13464605.html.

Watkins, Michael. 2014. *Die entscheidenden 90 Tage. So meistern Sie jede neue Managementaufgabe.* 2nd ed. Frankfurt: Campus Verlag.

Web.de, Ratgeber, Auto & Mobilität. 2016. *Lange nicht bewegt: So wecken Sie Ihr Auto aus dem Winterschlaf.* December 4, 2017. https://web.de /magazine/auto/lange-bewegt-wecken-auto-winterschlaf-32658568.

Wegner, Daniel M., D. J. Schneider, S. R. Carter, and T. L. White. 1987. "Paradoxical Effects of Thought Suppression." *Journal of Personality and Social Psychology,* 53(1): 5–13. https://doi.org/10.1037/0022 -3514.53.1.5.

Wötzel, Rudolf. 2009. *Über die Berge zu mir selbst. Ein Banker steigt aus und wagt ein neues Leben.* Munich: Integral Verlag.

Zucker, Rebecca. 2021. "How Much Time Can I Take Off Between Jobs?" *Harvard Business Review.* October 27, 2021. https://hbr.org/2021/10 /how-much-time-can-i-take-off-between-jobs.

Acknowledgments

My thanks go to Prof. Dr. Veit Etzold, best-selling author and my former BCG colleague, whose support was so pivotal to realizing this book and without whom my proposal would never have made it to the publisher. He taught me how to write a story.

Thanks go also to Emilio Galli Zugaro, who has so often supported me in my journey as a coach. It was he who gave me the idea of writing this book over a glass of wine many moons ago.

Thanks to Markus Draeger: our evening in Cologne encouraged me to put pen to paper and finally get to work.

I want to thank Dick Tyler, Luca Regano, and Nick Phillis, who inspired me and encouraged me to try my hand as a writer on our shared trip to Lisbon.

Thanks go to Brigitta Wurnig, who told me up front that there was something she knew I needed to say. I believe she knew about this book before I did.

I wish to thank my former colleagues at Boston Consulting Group, who paved the way for the book to exist today. Thanks to Isabel Poensgen and Mirko Nikolic, my exemplary role models for the journey into coaching; Jan-Philipp Martini, who encouraged me to write beyond the confines of traditional strategy topics; and Bolko von Oetinger, who inspired me to put a book back on the shelf myself (BCG insiders will know what I mean).

Thanks to Anne Scoular and Carol Kaufman, who supported my development as a coach and writer by showing me how to take a closer look.

I want to thank Dr. Frank Thiele, a longtime friend from my Mannesmann days, who supported me with such encouragement and enthusiasm when I had the idea of writing a book.

Finally, deepest thanks go to my wife, Astrid Greiser, for her loving support and understanding when I disappeared to my desk for days and nights on end. She is the most important person in my life. Together with our two children, she reminds me each day what really matters.

About the Author

© Christian Amouzou

Christian Greiser is an executive coach and management consultant. He guides thought leaders, decision makers, and entrepreneurs on their personal development journeys, helping them figure out their values, talents, and strengths. As he does so, he brings not only his perspective as a senior strategy consultant with operational leadership experience, but also an intuitive understanding for the role of personality in business. Prior to establishing his own consultancy, Christian held the role of Senior Partner at Boston Consulting Group (BCG) and led one of the largest practice groups worldwide. An engineer by education, he occupied managerial roles at German industrial conglomerate Mannesmann AG before entering the world of consulting. He studied in Braunschweig, Paris, and London and is a Fellow of the McLean Institute of Coaching, an affiliate of Harvard Medical School.

Christian and his wife divide their time between the German town of Meerbusch, near Düsseldorf, and the Greek island of Corfu. Christian has been practicing meditation with Zen masters of Europe and Asia for more than fifteen years and is the founder of a global mindfulness network. Insights from this meditation practice are also incorporated into his coaching.

For more information, visit www.greiseradvisory.com.